# The Modern Shaman

## Shamanic Guide to Abundance and Relationships

by Antonio Siano

The Modern Shaman

**Author: Antonio Siano**

**Legal Disclaimer**

This text is provided for informational purposes only and in no way replaces the professional opinion of doctors, psychologists or other healthcare experts. Any references to scientific studies, alternative treatments, or "natural medicines" in this book should not be construed as medical advice or encouragement of the use of such practices.

Readers are strongly advised to consult a qualified professional for any physical, psychological, mental or emotional condition they may have before undertaking any practice or exercise mentioned in this text. The personal experiences shared by the author are not intended to be a substitute for professional medical advice, treatment, or diagnosis by qualified personnel.

The exercises proposed in this book are intended as educational tools and not as a substitute for medical or therapeutic treatments. It is recommended to perform these exercises in safe and calm conditions. In particular, it is important not to carry out the proposed meditations while driving or carrying out other activities that require full attention to avoid risks to personal safety and that of third parties.

# Contents

# Introduction

*"The best books are precisely those that say what we already know"*

~ George Orwell

## In Search of Hidden Potential

Have you ever felt that subtle restlessness, that suspicion that life has even more to offer you, without knowing how to make it happen? Perhaps, in a moment of tranquility, you found yourself daydreaming, imagining a different, fuller and richer reality. Have you ever wondered if there is a secret to a life of abundance and fulfilling relationships, and if so, how can you unlock it? These questions, which resonate in the depths of our soul, take us on a journey of discovery. Every step brings us closer to that version of ourselves we've always aspired to be, the one we perhaps dreamed of becoming as children. Along the way, for reasons we sometimes forget, we have lost that connection, becoming absorbed in the 'duties' of daily life. Knowing how to laugh at yourself and at life's little ironies can be the first step towards reconnecting with that part of us that, deep down, always knew there was more to discover.

## The Power of Being Yourself

The phrase "Nothing is more powerful than being yourself" first resonated with me at just 11 years old, during a time of family and financial crisis, which would affect my academic performance with the classic phrase: "it has a above average intelligence, but not committed." I didn't understand how I could combine my being with my school commitments, but I decided to learn a study method. Helped by my mother but in particular by my first sister Mariagrazia (considered in the family to be the scholar with excellent results) I began to understand how to delve deeper into study topics and at the same time be able to express my own style. My imaginative journeys in playing at being a rich and powerful but compassionate man who gave to the poor - I considered myself poor or at least among the NOT wealthy families - pushed me to look for what I could share with the world. "Desire for greatness" someone said, but inside me I felt that I was much more than what I could express.

At a time when it seemed like everything around me was falling apart, I discovered a simple yet revolutionary truth that shaped the rest of my life.

My name is Antonio Siano, but I'm not just that. I define myself as a serial entrepreneur and a modern shaman. I am a father, son, husband, brother, friend, musician, and many other things. Here, in our shared space, I will translate these abstract concepts into tangible principles and practical tools. I learned that I can be anyone without necessarily identifying with it. And, despite the profound issues we face, don't forget the power of the smile: it is the tool I use to face life lightly and which I hope will infect you too!

## A Shared Journey

Each of us is a traveler on this incredible journey called life, and the answers to your questions could be found right here, among these pages. Regardless of your culture, financial situation or background, "The Modern Shaman" invites you to explore the depths of your authenticity and unlock the unexplored potential that lies within you.

These words are the starting point of our journey. The questions that crowd your mind can finally be answered: What does "being yourself" really mean? How can we transform challenges into growth opportunities? Is it possible to live a life of abundance and create authentic, satisfying relationships?

Dive into an extraordinary journey with me, exploring together the foundations of strength, the curves of youth, and the lessons I've learned along the way. Each chapter will open a window into my life and, more significantly, reflect yours, offering you the key to discovering your hidden potential.

In my life, I have had the privilege of meeting many 'Masters', people who have shaped my being in unexpected ways and I hope you will meet them too through my words. This learning journey begins with my family - my parents, brothers and sisters - each of them has left an indelible imprint on my heart and mind. But the most significant inspirations came from my wife Rossella, to whom I recently gave the book "Tribe of Mentors" by Timothy Ferriss[1], writing to her in dedication: "You are the most important Master for me".

---

[1] Reference in the chapter "Bibliographical References"

It is in my sons, Alessandro and Riccardo, that I discovered the most enlightening Masters. Through them, almost like looking in a mirror, I can see myself and the areas where I can improve. Their intelligence, perseverance and perspicacity, which far surpass my own, are not only a source of admiration but also a powerful stimulus to my personal development. Listening to them play the piano or the guitar, realizing how gifted they are - and I affirm this with genuine admiration - not only fills my heart with pride, but also acts as a compass that guides me in the continuous effort to be their worthy travel companion. The lessons I learn from them every day enrich my life in ways I could never have predicted, and I want to share some of these precious discoveries in these pages.

To these words of recognition and admiration, I add a profound gratitude for being born into a family that provided me with solid roots and wings to fly. I extend this gratitude to my parents, brothers and sisters and also to the families they have created, enriching my life with my grandchildren. Every single member of my birth family, with their unique stories and shared lessons, has been an inspiration and a significant part of my journey.

My gratitude also extends to my wife's family: my sister-in-law, my mother-in-law and her father. Although my time with him was brief before his passing many years ago, she left a wonderful and lasting memory in my heart.

Thank you for being my compass, my safe haven and the stars that guide my path, enriching my existence every day with a depth and meaning that only family can offer. The presence of every member of my extended family in my life is a priceless gift, an ongoing source of learning, love, and joy. I am grateful for every moment shared, every smile exchanged, and every lesson learned alongside them. This extended network of family bonds taught me the importance of connection, mutual support, and unconditional love through their example and guidance.

Recognizing a Master in those around us is the first step in learning to know yourself. We can find constant inspiration in the people around us and in humanity's rich history. Every meeting is an opportunity for growth and reflection, a journey to discover who we really are.

I invite you to always keep this book at hand and consult it at different moments in your life, just as I was taught. Each stage of life brings different challenges and opportunities, and this book can be a valuable guide at every stage of your journey, a silent companion that will accompany you on your journey of inner discovery.

At the end of each chapter you will find exercises, identified by specific codes, which have been carefully designed to guide you. Codes evolve with your progress, they are a method of organization and represent a journey deep into your subconscious, revealing layers and aspects of you that perhaps you didn't even know existed. It is a sort of enigma, where each code to be deciphered is a key to access the most secret place where your True Essence is kept.

Apply these exercises for at least 21 days, keeping a diary of your progress and discoveries. This is an invitation to take time for yourself, nourish your soul, and cultivate the garden of your inner being. With each page and each exercise, you will have the opportunity to grow, to evolve, to blossom.

You will see how, step by step, you will begin to unlock and explore new horizons of your being. Are you ready for this adventure to discover authenticity, abundance and deeper relationships? Start this journey with me.

Together, we will walk through the valleys and mountains of your soul, discovering hidden treasures and illuminating forgotten corners of your heart. We'll discover how to turn challenges into triumphs, and how your true potential can illuminate every aspect of your life, bringing a radiant light to every step you take.

# Roots and Growth

*"Every adult has the heart of a child inside him."*

~ Antoine de Saint-Exupéry

## Childhood and Family

I was born in 1973 in a modest house in the province of Naples in Italy, immersed in a family environment full of love, but marked by economic difficulties. My childhood, although not easy, taught me valuable lessons that shaped my resilience and inner strength. Frequently, my mother Anna Maria told the origin of my name, a story that was always fascinating due to its extraordinary ability to involve me in her stories. They had initially chosen to call me Fabrizio, but the midwife, discovering that I would be one of two monozygotic twins with the second undeveloped fetus, proposed the name Antonio. It was the day of the celebration of Saint Anthony, and according to her, I looked like that saint's angel. The story of my name, chosen so suddenly, reflects the inscrutable and mystical nature of life that has always accompanied me.

Growing up in a large family, I learned the importance of human relationships and empathy. Despite some health difficulties and economic constraints, I have found a refuge and a means of expression in music. Early skill on the guitar, despite my tiny fingers, marked the beginning of my journey of self-expression and creativity. A passion which, however, I inherited from my mother, who had studied piano as a child. "I haven't touched the keys in years," she once told me with a wistful smile, "but every time I hear you play, it's as if the music cures me and I play with you too." Although over time she had put down the idea of playing, through us children she rediscovered and shared the power, even healing, of music.

## Music and Growth

Music has been the soundtrack to many events within my family. In fact my first older brother Vincenzo had taught me to hold the guitar as he himself is an excellent guitarist. I remember some evenings in which we organized real concerts in which each child contributed: Vincenzo on the guitar, followed by Lucio on the bass, my sisters Mariagrazia and Daniela on the harmony of voices and I, the youngest, the performer who often also sketches to make people laugh, and finally my parents: the paying public.

Laughter has always been my most powerful weapon, because I quickly understood that even in the most difficult situations, a good joke could at least change the perspective. In fact, to this day I use it even in the projects I carry out, as a useful tool for not taking oneself too seriously and above all for changing perspective.

Sensitivity and the ability to perceive the world in different ways, such as when I "talked to angels", have proven to be both a blessing and a challenge for me. I was 6 years old when I revealed to my mother my ability to communicate with the "angels of the house". She, a woman of the Catholic faith, while maintaining an open approach to the possibility of such phenomena, put me to the test. "Okay, show me." I concentrated so hard that, with the assistance of my "angel friend," the living room lights came on. My mother, struck by what happened, exclaimed: "don't ever do it again, it's dangerous to play with these forces!" Not long after, a new presence manifested itself in my parents' room: "Antonio, enough, promise me that you will no longer try to get in touch with these energies!".

From that moment, for a certain period, I no longer saw anything, I tried to concentrate on something else, orienting my childish thoughts towards other things. I didn't know that I was adopting a thinking technique that would serve me later in life.

## Aspirations and Reality

Growing up in times of sacrifice, where even the luxury of eating meat regularly seemed like an unattainable dream, taught me the value of resilience. My parents, despite the difficulties, dedicated themselves to our growth, trying to lighten the burden of the financial situation. This reality pushed me to make a promise to myself: one day I would become rich, to free myself from financial problems once and for all. As a child I played billionaire, and Daniela, my beloved "twin" despite the age difference, and playmate par excellence, represented the faithful subordinate who came to me for help. Daniela had this extraordinary ability to empathize with the role and convince me that her pleas were real, to the point of often making me burst into tears, and then looking at me and turning everything into laughter, reminding me that it was just "all a big show". Even today, we continue to mix serious themes with moments of pure childish lightheartedness, keeping everything incredibly light.

Valentino, my father, watched as we played, sometimes so thoughtful that I could see glimpses of future conversations. "Only criminals, politicians and all those who are willing to compromise their moral principles make the money." In his opinion, only hard work would guarantee a stable, safe and worth living life. I am sure that for him they were necessary recommendations to invite me to stay with my feet on the ground, to follow a purpose, not to associate with questionable people, but already by nature I was not attracted to that dark side and I only continued to dream of a life of prosperity.

The city where I lived, on the other hand, didn't help my thinking much; the presence of organized crime was evident, it oozed into every aspect of life. My father taught me to defend myself physically and to deal with daily challenges. While I was growing up, despite not having a wrestler's physique, I was rather skinny and lean; I managed to shape my body until I achieved good results with physical exercise.

I found judo to be the ideal sport to appreciate the discipline and, above all, the techniques that made me very strong. My teacher, Mario, was an incredible man; he didn't want to hear about fights outside the tatami. With him I learned to overcome the limits of physical resistance of my body and to understand the importance of the mind in confrontation with the opponent.

I couldn't realize then that the environment had forced me to learn to defend myself, but violence was not a part of who I really am at all. I had learned, in the wrong way, to be hard and intransigent, I engaged in unnecessary fights, an anger whose origin I did not want to recognize. I only understood with adulthood who I should have reconciled with, who I should have embraced and loved without reservations: myself as a child.

## Positive thought

These experiences of resilience and fighting against adversity, countering my father's beliefs and facing the realities of my hometown, laid the foundation for a deeper understanding of the power of positive thinking. Through the concepts expressed by Norman Vincent Peale in his book 'The Power of Positive Thinking'[2], which I have read several times, I learned, for example, how a positive approach to life, even in the most adverse circumstances, can cultivate resilience and optimism from a young age. I realized that my efforts to overcome obstacles and protect my child self were actually expressions of a positive approach to life that would shape my future.

You might think, 'Antonio, do I really have to listen to your childhood memories? I already have mine to deal with!' And I say: of course yes! Because every anecdote has its own little lesson, and if I can make you smile while I talk to you about my past, well, I'd say it's a double success! Each of us can draw on our childhood experiences to better

---

[2]Reference in the chapter "Bibliographical References"

understand who we are today. Our early years of life are crucial for developing resilience and courage, which are essential for facing future challenges. I invite you to reflect on your growth experiences, finding strength and inspiration even in the most difficult moments. Peale's philosophy on optimism and positivity, which I have embraced in adulthood, has strengthened my belief that our attitude towards life can significantly influence our reality. In my personal and professional journey, I have seen this truth manifest itself repeatedly. Optimism is not just a philosophy; it is a powerful tool that can transform our thoughts, our actions and, consequently, our lives.

Optimism was accompanied by another motto used by my father to motivate himself, but which he often referred to me: "I wanted, I wanted and very strongly I wanted". This phrase, famous work by Vittorio Alfieri[3], poet and writer of the eighteenth century, my father often repeated it to give me strength when faced with complex situations, underlining that when a person really wants something - and today I would add: and he believes it! -he can obtain it with willpower alone. Since I didn't have a clear understanding of willpower during my adolescence, I dedicated myself to self-learning about how the human brain works.

In my personal and professional growth journey, I have always valued the importance of neuroplasticity, the brain's ability to reorganize and adapt in response to new experiences. This concept, which I highlight in my course "Your Future is Now", found a vivid demonstration during one of my shamanic retreats, particularly in the experience with a participant named Marion.

_______________________________

[3]Reference in the chapter "Bibliographical References"

Marion, the queen of silence on our four-day retreat, was so reserved she could have won at hide and seek without even hiding. Every time I tried to talk to her, it was like trying to have a conversation with a mime. We all glimpsed the internal battles she was fighting, kind of like I did when I tried to avoid eating vegetables by hiding them on my sister's plate (unbeknownst to her!).

When we reached the last session of our retreat, the Ego-Transcendence Practice - a practice I developed - inspired by neuroplasticity (yes, that thing that allows you to learn to use a smartphone even if you are over 30), I decided to push Marion pushes her limits by asking her to play the guitar. She, with a resistance worthy of an action movie hero, finally agreed, like when you give up and eat the last slice of pizza even if you're already full. And boy, when she started playing, it was like witnessing a neuronal miracle: an awakening of old passions that slept like a hibernating bear. And who would have thought? Marion not only knew how to play, but she was a real rock star! Maybe next time I'll ask her to perform a guitar solo, perhaps dressed as Elvis.

We discovered that Marion had studied music as a child, but then hung up her guitar, probably alongside her dreams of becoming a rock star. After her retirement, her newfound love for music was like a source of inspiration.

And so, Marion shows us that thanks to neuroplasticity, we can rediscover parts of ourselves that we thought were lost, like remembering where we parked the car in a crowded shopping mall. Resilience and inner strength, cultivated through neuroplasticity, are not just personal qualities, but are gifts that we can share and teach.

Through the course, workshops and shamanic sessions, my goal is to inspire others to explore and value their past experiences, using them as transformation tools for a more fulfilling future. Like the notes of a guitar resonating in a silent room, so our past experiences, shaped by neuroplasticity, can create harmonies in our lives, transforming memories into a symphony of growth and resilience.

To consolidate the concepts explored in these first pages and bring them to life through your personal experiences, immerse yourself in an exercise that will take you back in time. And now, without further ado, I present to you 'The Time Code: Back to Children' - your ticket to an emotional trip down memory lane.

### *The Code of Time: becoming children again.*

This magical code will take you on a journey through time, taking you back to the time when you were a curious and wondering child. Through this extraordinary practice, you will have the opportunity to re-establish a special connection with your younger self, rediscovering the precious qualities and wonderful experiences that helped shape the extraordinary person you have become today.

### Step 1: Preparation

Find a Comfortable Place: Choose your favorite corner of the house, where no one can disturb you. A soft pillow, a cozy chair, or even a piece of flooring works great. To add an extra level of relaxation, consider playing some calm, tranquil music in the background. Something light and non-invasive, like nature sounds or gentle melodies, can help set the right mood for your mental journey. If you're feeling particularly adventurous, why not build a pillow hut, just like you did as a child? Relive that sense of magic and curiosity!

Relaxation: Close your eyes and take five deep breaths. Slowly inhale through your nose and then exhale through your mouth, as if you were inflating and deflating a giant balloon. Imagine that each breath takes away a little of the stress of the day.

## Step 2: The Time Machine

Imagine a Big Screen: With your eyes still closed, visualize a big movie screen in your mind. It's your private cinema, so feel free to add personal details – magic popcorn, someone sitting next to you?

Grab your Imaginary Remote Control: Feel it materialize in your hand, complete with glittering buttons to travel through time and memory.

## Step 3: Journey into the Past

Press Back: Press the rewind button on your remote. Watch as scenes from your life scroll backwards across the screen. Go back to a time in your childhood when you overcame some major difficulty. Maybe that day you learned to ride a bicycle without training wheels, or that time you built the tallest tower out of bricks.

Immerse yourself in the memory: now, focus your attention on that moment. Can you see more vivid colors? To hear the sounds around you? Maybe the smell of cut grass or the taste of a post-adventure snack?

**Step 4: Explore and Connect**

Who's with you: See who's with you at that moment. Maybe your parents, siblings, or an imaginary friend who has a great sense of humor. Notice how they interact with you and how they support you.

Feel the emotions: Now, let the emotions of that moment envelop you. Feel that feeling of triumph, the joy of innocence, and that little bit of pride at having overcome a challenge.

**Step 5: Return to the Present**

Return to the Here and Now: When you're ready, press the play button to return to the present. Feel free to stop along the way to enjoy more great memories.

Gradual Reentry: Begin to slowly move your toes and fingers. When you feel ready, open your eyes. Take a moment to express gratitude, one of the most powerful vibrations, for the relived memories and for who you are today, thanks also to your past. Finally, write down your experiences.

Remember, this time travel isn't just a trip down memory lane—it's a chance to embrace the child you were, recognizing the extraordinary qualities you've carried with you to this day. It's like meeting an old friend - your childhood self - and remembering all the adventures and lessons learned together.

# Hidden Harmonies

*'Study is like the light that illuminates the darkness of ignorance, and the knowledge that results from it is the supreme possession, because it cannot be taken from us even by the most skilled of thieves. Study is the weapon that eliminates the enemy that is ignorance. He is also the best friend who guides us through all our difficult times.'*

~ Dalai Lama

## Between Music and Computer Science

Adolescence is often a period in which passions and talents are defined. For me, it was the period in which music and IT became not just interests, but real points of reference. It was a time of unanswered questions and bold dreams. In that sea of uncertainties, music and computing became my compasses, guiding me through the storms of youth. In this scenario, where financial restrictions imposed their limits, the determination to independently explore and develop my skills emerged as a welcomed challenge.

"What do you want for your eighteenth birthday?", my parents asked me "a used car or a keyboard?". Well, the car would have been really handy where I lived but I had no doubts: "The keyboard!". It was the embodiment of an ambitious dream that beat in my heart. Every time I touched the keys, I felt a sense of freedom and infinite possibility.

I realize that that choice marked a turning point in my journey towards independence and self-expression. I developed my own self-taught method of playing the piano and turned it into a business, playing at events. A first step into the world of entrepreneurship, but also a metaphor for my self-development journey. With each note I got closer to my potential, something that each of us has and can be discovered through passion and perseverance.

In piano bars, especially during wedding celebrations, I found a space for my music and also a stage to observe and learn from the love and life stories of others.

In southern Italy, there is an ancient tradition in which on the wedding day a beautiful party is celebrated that can last the whole day, with abundant food, music and unfortunately a lot of alcohol. Playing at weddings was certainly a commercial activity, but also an experience that immersed me in the joy and celebration of love. Each wedding was a different story, a new set of emotions to capture and express through music. In addition to this, I learned what it means to be of "service" to others.

In one of these weddings, which took place in a sumptuously decorated room, with garlands of flowers hanging from the ceilings and twinkling lights creating an almost fairy-like atmosphere, a curious little boy with a cheek that would have embarrassed a politician in election campaign, he decided it was time to make his big debut in the world of music.

With the confidence of a general going into battle, his small face lit up by a mischievous smile, he approached the piano and, without hesitation - and without asking permission - began to play a key. Yes, just one button. The result was a "tune" that was a mix between a Morse signal and an avant-garde piece. He wasn't exactly Mozart, but he certainly had the courage of a lion!

I wanted to engage in an improvised duet with this young prodigy, but he had turned that single key into a declaration of musical war. At every attempt I made to involve him in a more complex piece, he responded with a proud look, his cheeks flushed with emotion and a fanatical adherence to his key. Ding, ding, ding.

Finally, with a smile that hid my internal desperation, a mixture of admiration for his spirit and anxiety at the growing embarrassment, I politely asked him to give way to the professional pianist. His reaction? A miniature Shakespearean drama: tears, accusatory looks and guests who made me feel like a cartoon villain.

After the song, I approached the little rebel's table, ready for a truce. His eyes shone with a challenge that had just begun. Sitting next to him was his father, whose arched eyebrows betrayed a mixture of irritation and pride.

What followed was a scene worthy of a comedy. "My son has to play!" the father ordered, pronouncing those words with a threatening tone. All I had to do was invite the "prodigy" to the piano again. "Okay, put your fingers here and play with me" I replied, trying to explain to the child that playing that single note didn't really constitute a melody, but my attempts proved in vain. After a quarter of an hour of explanations, the response was a defiant look and the obstinate repetition of the same button: an incessant ding, ding, ding.

Fortunately, the time for the toast arrived, and the child was called back to his table. As I raised my glass, I reflected on the bizarreness of the situation, its unintentional humor, and the life lessons hidden in these small moments of chaos. After the first glass, the father offered me a second which seemed inevitable, but I, true to my mantra of moderation, politely declined. The father's reaction? "Drink!" he scolded me, getting annoyed by my refusal.

I grabbed the glass and simulated a sip; just at that moment, he got distracted. Taking advantage of the moment, with a feline sprint, I emptied the contents into the pot of a nearby plant. The father, satisfied, gave me a pleased smile. As I have learned over time, a sincere laugh and a warm smile have the power to transform tense moments into memories that will remain imprinted forever. And so, the party continued, with laughter, music and a little virtuoso who, with his grin, was probably already planning his next "performance"- or victim! A reminder that, in life, the strangest situations can be the most memorable, and that a good laugh truly is the best medicine.

This strong determination, rooted in the teachings of my parents, has always kept me away from excess, a beacon that guided me even in the darkest moments. And so, there was no room for illicit substances, nor for alcohol. Or perhaps it would be more accurate to say that I could indulge in a few drinks, but only up to a certain point, beyond which my stomach rebelled. In particular, the prospect of losing control over my body made a strong impression on me.

Looking back on those years, I now understand how every note I played was a part of my growth as a musician and an essential piece in building who I am now, a mosaic of experiences that shape my being. Sometimes that ding, ding, ding still resonates in my mind generating a pleasant laugh.

Within my family, a series of significant events marked the course of my adolescence, strengthening my passions and rooting them more deeply in me. Music and computing, still in their infancy at the time, were more than just interests; they were windows into new and exciting worlds.

But there was something else, an experience that went beyond the tangible. During the silent nights, an innate sensitivity allowed me to 'see' beyond appearances. These perceptions were a source of fear, but also of wonder, pushing me into a deep inner search. I held this secret, a burden I carried alone, until I crossed paths with my friend's grandmother, a medium renowned for her extraordinary abilities. So the day I met her came.

The medium's room was a sanctuary of mystery. The walls were adorned with old black-and-white photographs and enigmatic symbols. In the center, a flickering candle danced, casting shadows that seemed to take on a life of their own. The air was filled with a sweet, spicy scent, evoking images of distant places and ancient times.

"Boy, you look like you saw a ghost!" Grandma exclaimed with a good-natured smile, her eyes shining with unfathomable wisdom. I replied with a nervous laugh. "Maybe I did," I said in a small voice.

"Come, sit down," she said, pointing to a chair next to the table. As I sat down, Grandma continued, "Souls, you know, have a way of making themselves heard. They are like the wind whispering through the leaves or a shadow passing in the twilight. They only manifest when you think of them."

With eyes wide with curiosity and a hint of fear, I listened carefully. "But how can I know if it is really a soul speaking to me, and not just my imagination?" I asked with a mixture of skepticism and hope.

My grandmother, with one of those smiles that seem to contain centuries of knowledge, said to me: "Ah, my young friend, souls speak the language of the heart. They do not hide behind words, but reveal themselves in feelings, in intuitions, in dreams. You will feel the difference."

That day, I left the medium's room with more questions than answers. But deep down, I felt that something in me had changed. I didn't immediately understand her words, but as the years passed, I began to understand their true meaning.

Over time, I learned to listen to the silence and interpret the whispers of the wind. I understood that every thought, every memory evoked, was a bridge to those souls I had thought were lost. And in that bridge, between the visible and the invisible, between the past and the present, I began to find a sense of peace and connection with the universe around me.

These experiences, initially confusing and frightening, over time became a source of inspiration and insight. Every encounter with the inexplicable taught me to look beyond the visible, to explore the boundaries between the real and the imaginary. Indeed, these lessons have influenced my creative approach in music, computing and business, teaching me that there is always more than meets the eye.

This chapter of my life, full of development and challenges, was crucial in shaping the man I have become. It taught me not to fear the unknown, but to embrace it as a gateway to new understandings and possibilities.

## Work and Resilience

Every summer during the school break, as a sort of ritual, I immersed myself in different types of work to accumulate a small treasure. Among these, being a lifeguard in a bathing establishment left an indelible mark. In addition to teaching me responsibility and caring for others, that experience introduced me to the many aspects of human interaction. I remember how every day offered its share of challenges: from children who played too far from the shore, to adults who often underestimated the dangers of the sea. In these moments, not only was my alertness tested, but also my ability to communicate effectively and with empathy.

In this context, I learned to recognize and appreciate the small joys of everyday life and the "present moment". A parent's grateful smile after timely intervention or the enthusiasm of children learning to swim were priceless rewards. These moments taught me that, despite difficulties, there is always room for positivity and gratitude.

I vividly remember a day when the waves were churning with unusual ferocity, and a young swimmer seemed to be fighting against their fury. To deal with that terrifying situation, I called upon the spirit of Mitch from "Baywatch" who took possession of me. I could already imagine the epic soundtrack as the background while, emulating his iconic slow-motion sprint, I headed towards the water, life jacket in hand. But what I recovered was a disproportionately large one, so cumbersome that it almost made me trip over myself. When I got close to the boy, I discovered that all he needed to save himself was to simply stand up. However, with an impulse worthy of the most melodramatic of rescues, I pulled him to shore, breathing with the short breath of the hero who never loses his composure. Undeterred, I proceeded with stage resuscitation, which was clearly superfluous. Another lesson learned: I now knew how to transform a moment of great fear, maintain clarity in stressful situations and be of service to others - and the importance of knowing how to laugh at oneself, in the face of the absurd theater of life.

These earnings were fun but I also wanted to lighten the burden on my parents. At the same time gain a greater understanding of the value of money and work. As the years passed, this experience made me appreciate my parents' sacrifice and commitment even more.

The biggest challenge, however, came from the temptation of easy money. It was a test not only of integrity, but also of self-reflection. One evening, while I was discussing with friends how to supplement my income, one of them proposed a 'deal' that guaranteed immediate earnings. I found myself reflecting not only on the possible consequences, but also on the values that my parents had passed on to me. I asked myself, 'This is the kind of person I want to become?' The decision to walk away from that offer wasn't just a rejection of a shortcut, but an important step in defining who I was and who I wanted to be.

Seeing friends take dangerous paths affected me deeply, leading me to question the motivations of such choices and my role in society. This awareness has strengthened the determination to pursue a path guided by the principles of integrity and responsibility. These experiences shaped not only immediate choices, but also my overall outlook on life, teaching me that resilience sometimes requires the courage to say no to safeguard one's values and those of the community.

## Decisions and Adaptations

Initially, I attended computer engineering at university, but was unable to complete it due to growing financial needs and my desire for independence. With empty pockets, but a mind full of ideas, I dedicated myself to creating new initiatives, always respecting the law. This experience taught me the value of self-reliance and the importance of thinking creatively when faced with difficulties.

My parents never neglected basic needs, such as food, school fees and clothing. Unfortunately, among these needs, the habit of cigarettes has arisen, which began during an act of adolescent rebellion at the age of sixteen. That first cigarette then became a constant companion, a silent shadow that followed my every step. Smoking is a true addiction, which requires significant awareness and effort to overcome. The struggle to free myself from this addiction, which occurred just twenty years later, was a battle of wills, a dance between desire and determination.

My youthful challenges, including paranormal experiences and the shadow of organized crime, required me to develop a resilience and ability to adapt that have proven essential in my life, both personal and professional. These episodes taught me to stay open to unorthodox possibilities and explore beyond the boundaries of the normal but most importantly to listen to my inner voice and trust my perceptions.

Although I did not complete my computer engineering education, the foundation I gained there laid the foundation for my self-directed development. It was an unfinished chapter, but full of lessons, which prepared me for the entrepreneurial challenges I would face.

I have a special message for those seeking wisdom and inspiration: As you pursue your dreams, don't overlook the importance of formal education. Academic education lays the foundation for the methodology without which it will always be difficult to assimilate new concepts, just like when I was unable to express myself as a child. It is the basis for success, a springboard for self-education and personal development.

Although I did not complete my undergraduate education, the foundation I gained during that time was essential to my self-learning journey. For example, the basics of logic and mathematics learned at university helped me develop a methodological approach in my entrepreneurial projects.

Many successful entrepreneurs and leaders dedicate a significant portion of their earnings and time to continually enriching their knowledge. This happens through courses, mentorships, shamanic retreats, webinars and various forms of self-learning.

By sharing my experiences, I hope to inspire not only young readers, but all those who boldly pursue their passions. I urge them to trust their unique abilities and see every obstacle as a valuable opportunity to learn and grow.

In the glitzy world of social media, success stories are often presented with an aura of ease and immediacy. Glittering outlines paint a picture of effortless triumphs, where every success seems to be achieved with a simple click. However, this narrative leaves the deepest truth in the shadows: the path to success is dotted with dedication, perseverance, continuous commitment but above all in believing in one's dreams and having the courage to follow them.

Much of what is perceived as 'instant success' actually hides countless hours of invisible work: sleepless nights, self-taught study, defeats, moments of doubt and uncertainty. These fundamental aspects of the journey to achieving goals are rarely highlighted in the stories told on social media.

In this digital age, where appearance can overwhelm substance, it is crucial to recognize that success is not a sudden achievement, but rather a gradual process. This perspective pushes us to look beyond the glossy facades of social media, valuing the journey and authentic commitment behind every success story, regardless of its public recognition.

This awareness, that universal knowledge is available to everyone but that knowing how to access it is a privilege reserved for a few, represents a principle that has constantly illuminated my path. As Benjamin Franklin once said, 'An investment in knowledge always pays the greatest interest.' These words resonated within me, spurring me to invest in cultivating my garden of knowledge, not only for myself, but to share its fruits with others.

## Life lessons

So, you're still here with me, huh? Good boy! Now, guess what? After childhood and adolescence, what comes next? That's right, adulthood! But don't run away yet, I'm not just telling the movie of my life for the sake of it. There's a method to my madness, I promise! You might ask yourself, 'Do I really have to listen to this whole story? Haven't I had enough of my troubles already?' And I reply: 'Absolutely yes, because sometimes in other people's stories we discover ideas for solving our own intrigues!'"

Let's see together how thoughts are prepared in the kitchen of the mind. Why do you think the way you think? Where do those brilliant or less brilliant ideas that float around in your head come from? Here, we are about to uncover the pot and discover the secret recipe!

***The Reconnection Code: Your Passions.***

Hey, remember Marion? The one who picked up the guitar again and felt like a rock star at retirement? That's right, we're about to do something similar. But this time, let's go back to our teenage days. Yes, those days of exploration, of first crushes, of loud music. Before diving into our teenage return, let's reflect for a moment. Neuroscience tells us that reliving past emotions and experiences can activate parts of our brain linked to creativity and joy. This is because, during adolescence, our emotional and sensory experiences are particularly intense and formative, creating strong and long-lasting neural connections[4]. Reliving those teenage emotions is fun and can also actually reinvigorate creative thinking by bringing you back to those parts of yourself that you may have forgotten. So, even if it seems a little crazy, dive into this exercise with the confidence that you are doing something good for your brain and your spirit. Ready to relive adolescence and awaken the teenager within you?

**Step 1: Teen Set-Up**

- Find your secret corner, that place where you hid to listen to music or daydream.

- Grab your diary – yes, the old fashioned one, not the app on your smartphone!

---

[4]Reference in the "References" chapter

## Step 2: Teenage Flashback

- Close your eyes, put on your headphones (if you like) and let the music of your 'teen' years transport you back in time.

- Think about the things you loved as a teenager. Those comics, that video game, that band, that weird hobby that only you understood.

## Step 3: Discover 'Retro'

- Now open your diary and write down everything that came to mind as a teenager. Come on, like in those sleepless nights spent writing down thoughts and dreams.

## Step 4: Rediscover 'Epic'

- Choose one of these passions. Something that made you feel unique, rebellious or just happy.

- Plan an 'epic' activity to relive that passion. Like playing that old guitar, drawing like a manga artist, or doing that skateboard trick.

## Step 5: 'Teen Style' Action

- Commit to doing this 'teen style' thing. Put your adult side aside for a moment and make room for pure fun.

- Every time you do this activity, write down in your diary how you feel. Yes, just like you did as a teenager.

**Step 6: Debrief 'Cool'**

- After a few weeks, read your diary and reflect: how has this return to your origins changed you?

- Think about how you might integrate this 'teen' passion into your adult life. Maybe there's something that teenager in you can teach today's adult.

This exercise is both a way to rediscover old passions and an invitation to let go of responsibilities for a moment and reconnect with the light-heartedness and curiosity typical of adolescence. As Marion demonstrated, rediscovering a passion can open new doors and energize our daily lives.

# The Art of Doing Business

*"To fail is not to fall; to fail is to stay where you fell."*

~ Socrates

## Success and Failure

In the journey of entrepreneurship, I have found that every step, whether a triumph or an obstacle, is a crucial note in the career symphony. As in a musical composition, where harmonies intertwine with dissonances to create a fascinating melody, my entrepreneurial journey has proved to be a fabric of successes and failures. The experiences, full of lessons learned, have shaped the understanding of the importance of being flexible, evaluating risks wisely and showing resilience in the dynamic world of business. This chapter is not just a chronicle of events, but an intimate diary of precious lessons, a testimony of how every failure, like a false note, can be traced back into a harmonious symphony of growth and success.

The entrepreneurial adventure began at the age of twenty-two, when, driven by a passion for music and the art of entertainment, I founded my first business: an intermediation agency in the world of entertainment. Inspiration came from my musical performances, which gave me a glimpse of the many faces of the entertainment universe. Like a game of Tetris, the company expanded rapidly, adding new pieces to the puzzle: from children's entertainment, to magician and clown shows, to supplying male and female models for nightclub events.

My partner and I were like two musicians playing in perfect harmony; every move we made felt like the right one, and the company flourished under this synergy. However, as in any interesting story, there was an unexpected twist. A series of unexpected challenges arose, forcing us to close the doors of this promising venture. It was a moment of reflection, similar to a pause in a musical composition, marking the end of a chapter but the beginning of a new movement.

In this chapter, I share with you not only the chronicle of these events, but also the valuable lessons I learned from them. I learned that entrepreneurship requires the ability to adapt and turn obstacles into opportunities, much like an artist finding new avenues of expression in the face of unexpected limitations. This approach to business, which mixes creativity, strategy and a pinch of audacity, has become the centerpiece of every new initiative I undertake.

Thus, I invite you to follow me in this story of experiences, to discover together how difficulties can be transformed into precious lessons, just as dissonant notes in a symphony can enrich its overall beauty.

## Radical Changes

I decided to make a drastic change and moved to Milan, in northern Italy, in search of new challenges and opportunities in the world of emerging industries. Until then, I hadn't traveled much. So, taking a trip of about 800km felt like going to another world.

At the beginning I felt like the emigrants from Southern Italy in the early twentieth century towards America but in reality I was just a few hours away from it. Everything seemed so different and new to me. New ways of speaking, new ways of enjoying coffee, different foods (before the gap between regions was much more noticeable). However, all this fascinated me, I wasn't scared at all also because I kept thinking "if I survived my city, I'll make a splash here!".

In that period, Lucio, my second eldest brother offered me a temporary refuge in his house not far from Milan, where he lived with his family. Those six months represented an important moment not only for the consolidation and ultimately the better knowledge of my brother, but also because an indelible bond was created between us with my beloved nephews, a relationship that continues to shine with intensity over the years. years.

Opening your heart to change can lead to unexpected encounters, transforming everyday life into something magically extraordinary. In that transition period, where every day was a step towards the unknown, I found, almost by chance, a traveling companion who I had already met in the carefree days of youth. She was a girl living in a town two hours away, a familiar face in a sea of new beginnings.

As if guided by the stars, this girl found a job in a well-known company and moved to Milan. Her destiny, she seemed to be designing her paths so that our paths might cross again. Even today, I smile at the memory of those first days together with Rossella, the girl who, from a guest in my life, transformed into my lifelong companion. I often joke with her, telling her that from that day she walked into my home, she captured my heart and never left.

From that day, Rossella became not only my beloved wife, but also the soul mate with whom I shared every adventure, every challenge and every joy. Together, we have woven a web of precious memories, living a life filled with unforgettable moments. Our bond has grown and flourished over the years, demonstrating that, sometimes, the truest and deepest love is born unexpectedly and is rooted in the very fabric of our existence.

On the path to success, my career took off in an area that was revolutionary at the time: the world of digital copiers. This role as a sales representative at a dealership was not just a job, but a launching pad for my aspiration to excel. With a hunger for success burning within me, I immersed myself in relentless study, determined to become an unparalleled communicator and marketer. The key? Know my product in every detail. This was not just a strategy, but a philosophy: knowledge is power, and this power turns challenges into opportunities.

But I didn't stop there. Boldly, I began recording my voice during sales, analyzing every word, every pause, every response. This self-examination was not an exercise in vanity, but a journey of self-discovery: learning from my mistakes, capitalizing on my strengths. Is the result? Awards, recognition, and a permanent contract with the parent company. This was the fruit not only of commitment, but of the desire to continually grow and improve.

Becoming a manager of franchise dealer agents was the next chapter in my story. In this role, I had the opportunity to shape the future of others, to instill the art of selling, to ignite the spark of passion and aspiration in those who were ready to listen. And then, as an even bigger step, I became a sales trainer in the multinational's prestigious in-house academy. Using the techniques I had honed on myself, I began to mold new talent, developing their communication, interest-building and team management skills.

Everyone's story is not just a personal journey, but a beacon of inspiration, a powerful reminder that the courage to embrace change can transform our reality. My ever-evolving career has led me to take on increasingly important roles, challenging me to broaden my horizons and push myself beyond my limits. On this journey, one day, an unexpected opportunity knocked on my door: the proposal from an owner of the dealerships I worked with, fascinated by my innovative vision, to create an online portal for the sale of corporate stationery products.

It was just the beginning of a new chapter, a turning point that led me to recognize the need to acquire more advanced managerial skills, which I found in the context of well-structured companies. Returning to the role of employee in an IT services company was not a step backwards, but a leap forward in my growth path. The transition from selling products to selling services was not easy; it was a revelation. Selling a product is tangible, immediate, but selling a service? It's about selling a vision, a dream, that the customer will see come true over time. And in this, I learned the art of building trust and communicating the intangible value of what we offered.

Shortly afterwards I had the opportunity to meet the top manager of a multinational company, and from that moment I was entrusted with the responsibility of managing an entire business unit. This unit comprised a team of 300 people providing in/outbound call center services to businesses. Although I was only twenty-nine years old, this experience was not only a challenge, but also a significant life training that prepared me for the boldest step up to that point in my career: the foundation of my own call center.

The audacity. This was the spark that lit the fire of my business. It was a courageous decision, taken at a crucial moment, which proved that fear is not an obstacle, but a stepping stone to success. Every step of this journey has strengthened my belief that no matter where you start, your determination and ability to adapt are the keys to unlocking unimaginable potential. Your story is your power. Use every experience, every challenge overcome as a step towards the realization of your dreams. You are the captain of your ship, and the ocean of success awaits you.

To reduce costs, I decided to relocate part of the call center to Moldova, considering the ease of communication due to linguistic proximity. I remember my first trip to the capital Chisinau, an adventure that began with a flight in a twin-engine plane that ticked more than a retired Swiss watch. The air link, which passed through Romania, was famous for being less reliable than summer weather in England. Sitting at the airport in Timisoara, surrounded by a landscape that looked like a large snow-frosted cake, we waited six hours for departure. And when I say 'snow', I mean real snow, not the kind you sprinkle on Christmas sweets.

Finally, we set off in a twin-engine plane that seemed to have as much desire to fly as I do to run a marathon. And to add a touch of the surreal to the trip, I had a very special flight companion. No, I'm not talking about a celebrity or a famous influencer, but about a chicken. Yes, just a chicken, in a small cage placed on the legs of my seat neighbor. She occasionally stared at me with a look that seemed to say, "You too, huh? You'd rather be somewhere else." I have to admit, though, that her unexpected presence turned that flight into an unplanned comedy. Every time the twin-engined plane lurched, and our 'feather crew' commented with an indignant cooing, I couldn't help but laugh.

Looking back, that chicken was perhaps the best traveling companion I had ever had. At least she wasn't occupying the armrest and chatting incessantly about her latest trip to the tropics. And, most importantly, she taught me that sometimes, even in the strangest and most stressful situations, a good dose of humor can turn a potentially terrifying experience into an anecdote worth telling for years.

Arriving in the capital, I found myself immersed in a sea of possibilities and unknowns. As I wandered through the still bare offices, my mind worked frantically to give shape to the project I had in mind. Every staffing interview, every decision about office space, every choice of equipment needed felt like a piece of a larger puzzle, a puzzle I was meticulously assembling.

As the days passed, the experiment became reality. It was amazing to observe how quickly people absorbed and interpreted the scripts we had prepared in impeccable Italian. This rapid learning ability and their dedication were not only a confirmation of my instincts but also of the untapped potential of these individuals. The satisfaction of seeing the project grow was palpable, so much so that new doors soon opened: two offices, one in Milan and, curiously, the other right in my city, Naples.

However, just when everything seemed to be going according to plan, fate had another unexpected twist in store for me. The success, which I had barely tasted, turned out to be ephemeral. My partner, the one with whom I had shared not only the enthusiasm but also the challenges of the foundation, decided to sell a branch of the company that was bigger than him. This unexpected movement called into question the future of everything we had built together.

In this whirlwind of events, however, there was a decisive turning point. It was in that period of uncertainties and reflections that I crossed paths with people who were fundamental and decisive for my future. A meeting that marked the beginning of a new adventure, an adventure that would prove to be one of my greatest successes.

## Between Luxury and Reflection

In the meantime, I had started a small company that aimed to connect European companies with Chinese companies. It all happened during the early days of Alibaba when she was not yet well known in Europe. I dedicated myself to exchanging specific products. Companies came to me with requests for unique items, such as a particular type of bolt that was not difficult to produce but expensive in Europe. They sent me the details of the project and through a network of professional contacts, I sent it to manufacturing companies in China. Once the product was made, I imported it for my client. I also used outside companies to monitor the quality control process, logistics and more. This experience taught me a lot about manufacturing processes, importing products from Asia, and much more.

One day, a friend with whom we still exchange deep and sincere messages, informed me that one of his clients, an important player in the energy sector who sold electricity to businesses and private individuals, wanted to create a campaign to promote electricity. energy efficiency. They planned to give away two energy-saving light bulbs to their customers, as LED lighting was not yet widespread and these bulbs were a significant improvement over traditional tungsten filament bulbs. It took me about a year to find the right supplier with the right prices. A commitment that marked the first time I reached one million euros in turnover. Over the next two years, turnover grew significantly.

However, this success opened my eyes to the world of electricity, specifically the opportunity for greater demand for renewable energy sources. The idea of combining business with something truly beneficial for the planet has always fascinated me. Earn money while also contributing to the common good! Yes, because I was, and am, still convinced that the transition towards increasingly less polluting sources of electricity represents the true path to sustainable coexistence with Mother Earth.

"If you want to get first, run alone, if you want to get far, walk together" says an ancient African proverb and I found in Massimo the ideal partner to go very far. Complementary characters - how much patience he had with me and I with him - linked by a deep brotherly affection, together we founded a company that aimed to involve investment funds and large users, offering design and management services for the authorization process for plants large-scale photovoltaics (utility scale). Due to the huge demand at the time, we turned into an EPC contractor, meaning we started building these installations ourselves. Our expansion has been rapid and we have opened offices in several European countries, even venturing into the United States with an office in Philadelphia. We reached turnover peaks of over 50 million euros per year and our initial team of three employees grew to a peak of 700. It was an intense period and, for the first time, I entered the world of "luxury".

I was living exactly the dream I had as a child: a luxurious house, prestigious cars (sometimes even with chauffeur!), holidays in postcard places. I was under forty and living the life of a millionaire, although I wasn't accumulating the same wealth. I felt a voice growing inside me, soft but persistent, reminding me of the cost of all this. Endless hours of work, a walking pharmacy in my briefcase, and the suffocating realization that I was missing out on precious moments with the people I loved. My children were growing up, and I wasn't there.

During that time I understood that true luxury is not found in material objects, but in shared moments, in family laughter, in the warmth of a home full of love. This realization rocked my world, bringing me to a crossroads: I could continue on this golden road or find a path that allowed me to be truly present in the lives of the people I cared about most. This was my deepest reflection, a passage that marked both my professional success and my inner journey towards a more balanced and authentic life.

## The turning point

The turning point came like a bolt from the blue at the age of thirty-seven. I had just returned from a holiday, a moment of apparent serenity, when I was struck by a microheart attack. This event, although it did not leave serious physical consequences, was a wake-up call that echoed loudly in my mind and heart. I was faced with an inescapable truth: the path I was on was not sustainable. Inspired by the unconditional love and purity of my two little treasures, my one and two year old sons at the time, I found the strength and courage to quit smoking, a change I achieved on the first try with a all personal and perhaps, one day, the subject of another story.

But the real crucial moment, the one that profoundly affected my spirit and soul, came with the death of my mother.

As I said goodbye, next to her in her last breath, I heard a familiar sound. It was the same as the moment when years earlier, my children in 2008 and 2009, saw the light of the world. Their first breath had a particular melody, a note that my musical ear would never forget. Years later, hearing it again in my mother's last breath I had the revelation that life and death are like two notes of the same melody, an eternal cycle that unites us all. It was a harmony that permeated my being and pushed me to search for deeper meaning in life.

On the day of my mother's funeral, my wife revealed a surprising coincidence to me. During the plane journey to reach me, she found herself sitting casually - but the case does not exist - next to some managers from my company, who had also left to attend the farewell, who were discussing among themselves possible financial problems that the company they felt should have addressed, revealing important concerns that they had not shared directly with me.

This fortuitous meeting was a sign for me, a warning from the universe that made me understand that we were about to face a possible serious financial crisis. I therefore decided to take the initiative, restructuring the company and investing in the sector of large-scale photovoltaic systems. The plan proved to be fruitful but not enough to protect us from one of the most unpredictable events in the business landscape: radical and retroactive changes in a country's legislation. The energy policy choices led to a collapse in the value of the plants. Customers stopped paying, and our company filed for bankruptcy in 2013.

It was a dizzying and sudden fall, in less than a year everything I had built vanished like snow in the sun. I found myself penniless and feeling lost, scared and filled with anger towards the entire world. During that time, I reached the lowest point of my existence and even seriously considered ending my life. However, it was in the depths of this desperation that I understood a fundamental truth: I did not desire death, but I desperately yearned to live an authentic life, a life that I had lost among the illusions of material success.

Although I was devastated by the defeat, I understood that I had to face this challenge with all of myself. My relationship with my wife was on the brink. I was constantly living in nervousness, uncertainty and the inability to see things clearly.

During the golden age, I was completely focused on money and power, convinced that I could shape the world to my will. This selfishness had closed the door to my emotions and soul that had supported my entrepreneurial successes.

So, what did I decide to do?

Before we continue, I want to share a direct message with you, from the bottom of my heart to yours. The road to success, remember, is littered with challenges and failures, but it is precisely in this rough terrain that life's most precious lessons are hidden. Imagine talking to a scientific researcher: he knows that of a thousand experiments, perhaps only one will lead to a revolutionary discovery. Yet, he never gives up, because every failed attempt is one more step towards knowledge. In this spirit, I want to inspire the entrepreneur within each of us to see every challenge as a stepping stone to personal and professional growth. Every obstacle faced is a unique opportunity to acquire new skills, broaden our vision and ultimately emerge wiser, more skillful and resilient than before.

This road, dotted with obstacles and triumphs, is more than just a journey; it is a spiritual pilgrimage that we all face. It is a journey that calls us to tune in to our inner voice, that voice that reminds us of who we really are beyond appearances and titles. It requires courage, determination and an open mind, not only to learn from external experiences, but also to listen to the silent lessons of our spirit. There is a phrase, the origin of which escapes me, that has always resonated in my mind, "Think big and you will become big!" and it is more than a mantra; it is a call to reconnect with our True Essence, that part of us that knows there are no limits to what we can achieve. This path is an invitation not to limit your vision, to dare, to dream beyond the boundaries of the possible and to work hard, but above all to remain faithful to your deepest essence, the one that knows that every dream born from the heart is already a reality in waiting to manifest itself.

### *The Winner's Code: Unlock Your Infinite Potential*

This exercise is a path designed to help you explore and overcome challenges by turning them into stepping stones for your future success. It is intended to be a retrospective analysis and journey of personal discovery that will allow you to unlock and harness your infinite potential.

Each of us, throughout life, encounters moments of difficulty and apparent failures. This path is not just an exploration of difficult moments and an invitation to connect with your inner voice to discover the deeper meaning of your experiences. Every obstacle you encounter is an opportunity to grow not only professionally, but also spiritually, rediscovering the values and beliefs that guide your most authentic essence.

This exercise will guide you through four key steps: Reflecting on Failure, Analyzing the Causes, Extracting Valuable Lessons, and Creating an Action Plan.

Through this process, you will be asked to look back with honesty and courage, identify the causes of your challenges, and draw crucial lessons from them. But the most important is the fourth step: creating an action plan based on these learnings. This step will transform your past experiences into a driving force for the future, allowing you to move forward with greater confidence, awareness and preparation.

The goal of this exercise is to help you recognize that every difficulty - in any area of your life - is an opportunity for growth, that every obstacle is a step that brings you closer to your goal. In fact, it also represents a concept that I greatly exalt: the ability to be an observer of one's Ego. By observing your mistakes without any emotional attachment and learning from them, you not only avoid repeating them, but you move with greater confidence and preparation towards your future goals.

Remember, success is not defined by the lack of challenges, but by your ability to overcome them and learn from them. "Think big and you will become big" is not just a motto; it is a philosophy of life that invites you to embrace your journey with optimism and determination. Now, dive into this exercise and start unlocking your infinite potential!

**Step 1: Reflection on Failure**

Description: Begin by taking a moment to reflect on a failure you have experienced. This may be a time when you faced a significant challenge or had a disappointing result.

Instructions:

Write a brief description of this failure, focusing on the facts and outlining the contours of the event without getting too emotional. What happened? What were the main circumstances? When did it happen?

**Step 2: Cause Analysis**

Description: Now analyze the causes behind this failure. Be honest with yourself and try to identify the mistakes, unfavorable circumstances or bad decisions that led to that outcome.

Instructions:

Reflect on the actions you took or decisions you made that contributed to this failure. What could you have done differently? What were the main causes?

**Step 3: Extract Valuable Lessons**

Description: At this stage, ask yourself the crucial question: "What lessons can I learn from this experience?" As you reflect on these challenges, also consider how they can teach you valuable lessons about your relationships, especially those as a couple. The understanding and growth that comes from these moments can be powerful tools for building deeper, more meaningful connections with your loved ones.

Instructions:

Identify the key lessons you learned from this failure. What have you discovered about the importance of planning, resilience, effective communication, or listening to your intuition? How can these lessons be applied in your current career?

**Step 4: Create an Action Plan**

Description: Finally, based on the insights gained, create an action plan. Set clear and achievable goals, strategies to avoid repeating the same mistakes, and specific steps to capitalize on lessons learned.

Instructions:

Set concrete goals based on the lessons learned from your failure. How can you use these lessons to improve your journey? What are the practical strategies you can implement?

Make sure this action plan is proactive and helps you grow sustainably and develop greater self-awareness.

# Crisis, Reflection and Rebirth

*"We can't solve problems with the same kind of thinking we used when we created them."*

~ Albert Einstein

## From Chaos to Clarity

So what had I decided to do?

Within the chaotic whirlwind of my life, I was faced with a crucial choice: if I truly wanted to embrace life in all its fullness, I would have to start completely from scratch. In a moment of deep introspection, I asked myself what the very essence of human existence was, and I was reminded of the first human act at birth: the first breath, a breath of life that marks the beginning of every existence.

Reflecting on this, I remembered an observation made by one of my assistants some time earlier. She had pointed out to me how my breathing was often labored, even in moments of apparent calm. This simple observation opened my eyes to a hidden truth: my breathing, so shallow and hasty, was the reflection of a mind in turmoil, constantly at the mercy of the storms of life.

I began to understand that by improving my breathing, I could not only alleviate the physical symptoms of discomfort, such as my persistent insomnia and other ailments, but I could also achieve greater mental clarity. Conscious and controlled breathing could become my lighthouse in the chaos, a fixed point from which I could navigate the turbulent waters of life with a new awareness and serenity.

## The Power of Breath

It all started as a solo adventure, with no guides or manuals to light the way. I vividly remember the first time I closed my eyes and tried to listen to my breathing, to feel the flow of life flowing through me. For the first thirty seconds, it seemed like anything was possible; I was in harmony with the universe, a rare feeling of peace. But, like an elephant in a glass shop, my daily worries burst into the silence, messing up my tranquility with the subtlety of a tornado in a library.

Of all the challenges and shadows of that period, the darkest was that of a possible legal proceeding for fraudulent bankruptcy. A story which, due to its Kafkaesque nature, alone would deserve a separate book, which I would successfully resolve only ten years later, confirming my innocence. It was an omnipresent thought, the unwanted guest at a party, always ready to undermine the fun and ruin the atmosphere. Attempting to meditate in my home was like seeking calm at a rock concert: a nearly impossible feat, but not without a certain humor. Have you ever tried to undertake these exercises in the midst of domestic bustle, with two little musicians in diapers? Yes, my children have demonstrated an innate inclination for music from their very first months of life! My concentration was frequently interrupted by drum rolls, electronic toy melodies, children's songs and so on and so forth. Ironically, this chaos at home only fueled my determination to persist in daily exercise, with a tenacity that would have made even the most stubborn of mules proud.

In those days and weeks, each breathing session became a small theater of my internal conflict. One moment I was the Zen master, immersed in peace; the next moment, I was overwhelmed by thoughts that floundered like crazy fish in a pond. At some moments, the frustration became so strong that I had to stop exercising.

Yet despite these moments of discouragement, something in me refused to give up. Maybe it was that same tenacity that had helped me overcome past challenges, or maybe it was just the desire to prove to myself that I could do it. Whenever I felt overwhelmed by thoughts, I reminded myself that even the largest of trees begins as a small seed, and that each breath was a step towards growth.

Over time, I began to notice small changes: a sense of calm slowly creeping in, an ability to detach myself from anxious thoughts. This journey into the power of breathing taught me that even in total chaos, there is always room for a smile, for a moment of peace, and for the possibility of transforming challenge into triumph.

As I entered this new phase of my life, I began to notice a substantial change. The problems, rather than seeming like unstoppable giants, began to transform into simple obstacles, perhaps annoying, but no longer insurmountable. My perspective was changing: in every situation, instead of a dead end, I saw potential escape routes, and when these were not immediately visible, I began to trust that inner voice. It was that same voice that, like a wise spiritual mentor, had always whispered to me the path to joy and balance, even in my darkest moments.

## Windows of Wisdom

My self-improvement journey wasn't limited to breathing practice. I became an avid reader, devouring 1-2 self-help books a week. I discovered authors who were like alchemists of words: Napoleon Hill, Wallace Wattles, Ralph Waldo Emerson, William Atkinson, Eckhart Tolle, to name a few.[5] Each book was like an open window into worlds of unexplored wisdom.

At the same time, my passion for neuroscience provided me with a scientific framework to better understand how the mind works. It was like having an instruction manual for my brain, helping me crack the code of my habits and reactions. And then there was quantum physics, which opened the doors to an even more surprising reality, revealing the mysterious mechanisms that regulate the universe. Sometimes I felt like a new scientist who, with a mixture of

---

[5]Reference in the chapter "Bibliographical References"

amazement and disbelief, discovers that the world is much stranger and more wonderful than he had ever imagined.

Step by step, this knowledge helped me collect the fragments of the soul that I had unconsciously torn apart along the way. It was a bit like trying to put together a puzzle without having the reference image on the box, but with each piece I found my internal image became clearer and more complete.

On this personal journey of transformation it was as if I were drawing a map for anyone who was lost in the dark woods of despair and was looking for a path to the light. And on this journey, I learned that often the answer we were looking for is found not in great revelations, but in the small daily discoveries that lead us to a greater understanding of ourselves and the world around us.

## Mind-Body-Soul Integration

All meditation practices, shamanic ones, often emphasize the mind-body-soul connection, where emotional and psychological well-being can influence physical health. I realized that I was exploring territory that went far beyond simple relaxation or the search for inner peace. These practices emphasized a principle that I began to see as a fundamental truth of human existence: the inseparable connection between mind, body, and soul. It was as if I was discovering an ancient secret, hidden in plain sight, that would unlock the magic of perfect harmony.

Research in the field of psychoneuroimmunology, a word that could have won an award for complexity, became a source of profound inspiration for me. These scientific studies demonstrate that there is no clear dividing line between mental and emotional health and the immune system. I understood that the body was a symphony, and the mind, emotions and physical health were the instruments playing in perfect harmony.[6]For example, research from the University of California has shown that regular meditation practices can significantly reduce stress levels, improving the functioning of the immune system and reducing inflammation in the body.[7]

This understanding led me to see spiritual practices in a new light. They were feel-good exercises and powerful tools for enhancing physical health. It was as if I had discovered that, in addition to being the conductor of my own personal symphony, I could also tune the instruments to get the best possible performance.

I began to integrate this new awareness into my daily life. Every meditation, every mindful breathing session, every moment of connection with my soul became an act of care for my body. As if I were stoking a sacred fire within, a fire that burned away tension and invigorated every cell in my body.

Reflecting on this integration of mind, body and soul, I began to laugh as I thought about how, in the past, I had tried to separate these aspects of myself. I felt like I had been trying to run a marathon with one leg tied, without realizing that By freeing every part of me, I could run not only faster, but also with greater joy.

---

[6]Reference in the chapter "Bibliographical References"
[7]Reference in the chapter "Bibliographical References"

This new understanding was not just an abstract theory; it had become a vital part of my daily experience, from abstract theory to concrete. Every day, through these practices, I rediscovered the wonder of being a human being, a miracle of mind, body and spirit, perfectly intertwined in one harmonious unity. And in this harmony, I found the key to better health, and a richer, more satisfying life.

I also applied the lessons learned within the family: from aloe-based toothpaste without fluoride, to the most natural detergents possible, to dusting off our grandparents' ancient methods for treating a cold. These small gestures have contributed to creating a healthier home environment in harmony with nature.

Reflecting on this journey, I realize that every step, from breathing practice to reading enlightening books, represented a fundamental stage in my journey of rebirth. I also invite you, the reader, to consider how these practices can enrich and transform your life too.

### *Rebirth Code: Integration of Mind, Body and Soul*

This exercise is a spiritual and practical journey to rediscover your true self, a bit like a magician pulling a rabbit out of a hat, but instead, you bring out inner peace and harmony. It is designed to help you navigate through the chaos of everyday life with a smile, finding balance and awareness between mind, body and soul. The benefits? A mental clarity that makes you say "a-ha!", an internal calm that not even the best tea in the world could offer you, and a connection with yourself so deep that even your most hidden thoughts will want to come for a chat.

**Step 1: Conscious Reflection**

- Choose a quiet and comfortable place.

- Close your eyes and breathe deeply for a few minutes.

- Reflect on moments of crisis or difficulty you have faced.

- Write down your thoughts and emotions, trying to observe them without judgment.

**Step 2: Illuminating Reading**

- Read an excerpt from a self-help or personal growth book – yes, maybe from this beautiful, amazing, enlightening, amazing book you are reading now!

- Reflect on how the concepts you read apply to your life.

- Write down any insights or ideas that emerge from your reading.

**Step 3: Meditation and Integration**

- After reading, meditate silently, trying not to think about your favorite TV show.

- Imagine mind, body and soul waltzing together in perfect harmony.

**Step 4: Practical Action**

- At the end of the session, set a goal or action that reflects the integration of mind, body and soul.

- This could be practicing mindful breathing daily, reading regularly, or engaging in activities that nourish your physical and spiritual well-being.

- Record your progress and reflections in a journal.

Through this exercise, you will not only rediscover the wonder of being a complete human being, but perhaps you will also find that sense of inner peace that makes you smile as if you just heard your favorite joke. And, who knows, maybe the next time you hear about meditation, yoga, or mindful breathing, you won't be able to help but think, "Ah, that's what I was looking for!"

# Shamanism and Abundance

*"Magic is just science we haven't figured out yet."*

~ Sir Arthur Charles Clarke

### Reconnection with the self

As I was walking with my wife, immersed in memories of paranormal experiences, a spontaneous question escaped my lips: "You know, I would really like to know what a shaman is." He encouraged me to explore the ancient cultures of countries like Peru, Brazil or Colombia, so I started a Google search. Entering "shamanic experience", I was faced with the word "ayahuasca". After the first few lines I stopped scared, because I had always been distant from the use of chemical or psychedelic drugs. I had strong reservations, but I overcame the fear with further investigation, I felt an irresistible call, I wanted to know more.

That mysterious calling to my soul turned into the decision to attend my first ayahuasca retreat in 2015. Although it was an experience still shrouded in a veil of secrecy in many countries, including Italy, where ayahuasca is strictly illegal , I felt a deep call. That first ceremony was an epiphany that changed the course of my life forever. When I woke up, after the first night, I shared with amazement that I had glimpsed a layer of reality hidden beyond the ordinary one, a subatomic and energetic dimension. On that inner journey, I had navigated through it, understanding the texture of reality itself. I realized that ayahuasca could be a powerful tool to rapidly plumb the depths of my mind and reach the roots of conditioning ingrained since childhood.

I continued to participate in other retreats, discovering that my daily meditations, a practice I had followed for years, had intensified, becoming deeper and more effective. I was able to focus on specific problems, unraveling and untying them like intricate knots, thus arriving at their essence.

During the second retreat, I had the meeting that would profoundly shape my path: a traditional Colombian shaman, invited by the organizers to leave the Amazon jungle for the first time and fly to us. This encounter made me realize that if I wasn't ready for a journey into the jungle, the jungle itself would come to me. In a vision during that ceremony, I saw myself referred to by four shamans as their fifth companion. I didn't immediately understand the full meaning of that vision, but I sensed that it contained a profound message.

## Apprentice Shaman

I continued to dedicate myself to retreats, soon finding myself involved in the organization. I was entrusted with a seemingly modest task, but full of poetic meaning: cleaning the bathrooms. Armed with a broom and bucket, in the long hours of solitude between the vapors of the detergent and the glittering of the taps, I began to reflect. The silence, broken only by the splashing of the water, revealed to me that every gesture, even the simplest, hides a profound meaning, like a miniature work of art waiting to be enhanced. I therefore set myself a significant moral objective: to transform those long-neglected spaces into true temples of cleanliness.

That task soon became precious to me, there was a lesson in the meditative repetitiveness of the task and moreover it evoked childhood memories, when I observed my mother busy cleaning the house, busy making objects that were already shining shine. It was precisely from those experiences that my tendency to clean the kitchen until it was impeccable must have arisen, going over it not once, but twice! To lighten the monotony of work and keep my spirits high, my mother filled the room with stories and tales, many of which were figments of her lively imagination. It was in those moments that I understood how the talent of storytelling, which I so loved to use to fascinate my children with unpublished evening adventures, was a gift passed down to me from my mother, as precious as it was unexpected.

Daily interaction with dirt, far from the superficialities and demands of the business world, turned out to be the therapy I didn't need. I abandoned the mask of the successful entrepreneur I had crafted for myself, admitting that my vision was misguided, distant from reality and, more fundamentally, not in alignment with my true essence. In fact, people who achieve important business goals combine entrepreneurial vision and wisdom. Between the strong smell of ammonia and the delicate rustle of brushes, I rediscovered the meaning of a genuine existence: a return to my roots that flooded me with a simple and complete joy, echoing my mother's stories.

Later, I began to actively participate in shamanic ceremonies, exploring music with different instruments. Although over twenty years had passed since I last played a guitar, a central instrument in the Colombian shamanic tradition along with flutes and percussion, I felt that the music flowed naturally from me. I had the intuition that it wasn't me playing the instruments, but rather they themselves were playing through me. Learning these musical instruments turned into a meditation practice, making every note played a sound, a dialogue with the invisible with its own language beyond words. Music proved to be a powerful key to connecting the tangible world to the spiritual, acting as a bridge between the two. This journey of learning shamanic practices was intense and, although initially arduous, deeply rewarding.

During these ceremonies, I faced my insecurities and fears, discovering their deep roots. Each ceremony led to further understanding and integration of these experiences, establishing a psychological bond that enriched my spiritual journey.

On a promising occasion of exoticism and enlightenment during a retreat in Amsterdam, fate decided to play one of its strangest tricks. The shaman, the expected lighthouse of our experience, who was supposed to lead the ceremony, was struck by a sudden illness, leaving me in a sea of uncertainties. I was there, devoid of any pretense of shamanism, in front of a group of adventurous souls who had crossed mountains and valleys, as well as thinned their wallets, to immerse themselves in this experience.

The mix of fear and determination that pervaded me in that moment must have been something similar to what an actor feels when he forgets his line in the middle of a crucial scene, with the aggravating circumstance that in my case this time, there was no script. to follow. Yet, with unexpected courage, I found myself leading the ceremony. Every gesture I made, every word that came out of my mouth, seemed to be whispered by an ancient wisdom I didn't know I possessed.

A radical transformation occurred, suddenly all the internal experience learned up until then, combined with the humility of physical work, took on a fullness of meaning: I became a bridge between worlds. I felt the presence and encouragement of shamans I had met in my deep and personal journeys, as if their wisdom was flowing through me.

That experience proved enlightening, revealing an unexpressed ability: to be a conduit to something bigger and deeper than my existence. Thus began, almost by chance, my shamanic journey, a journey of mystery and discovery that continues to define my path.

## The Ritual

Witnessing a shaman prepare for a ritual is equivalent to watching an actor before going on stage, with the difference that, instead of Shakespeare, there is a touch of Amazonian magic. On the one hand, we perceive surrealism and a touch of comedy, and on the other, a deep respect for the mystical. Shamans, coming from different cultures such as Peru, Colombia, Brazil and Ecuador, wear hand-embroidered clothes, embellished with necklaces of seeds or animal teeth, symbols of their spiritual protections. Often, they complete their clothing with crowns that are not only decorative but also protective, especially for the head, which they consider a delicate part of the body.

Before my Dutch "debut", I participated in a ceremony conducted by a Peruvian shaman, during which I observed the use of a tied bundle of leaves, known as wayra. Initially, this tool seemed almost funny to me. I was like, "What do you do with that thing?" The profound understanding of this instrument was revealed to me through a difficult to explain visionary experience, in which I was able to "see" beyond the veil of material reality. It was in this way that I truly understood the energetic role of the wayra during the culmination of the ceremony, observing how the shaman used this tool to manipulate and direct the subtle energies within the sacred space.

The wayra, variously called Shakapa, Chakapa, Chacarpa or Huaira Sacha depending on the region, originates from the Quechua term and designates an instrument similar to a shaker, made with leaves of the Pariana genus. For example, in the context of the shamanic Inga tribe of the Colombian Amazon, the wayra is fundamental in ayahuasca ceremonies, where the curandero waves it around the patient while singing an icaro, a healing song. The sound of the wayra, generated by a wide range of movements, creates an atmosphere of energetic cleansing - also called "Limpia" in Spanish.

Some say they see ribbons of light floating around the wayra during rituals, creating an almost magical atmosphere. Traditionally, wayra is made by tying leaves to form a fan-shaped instrument, which produces soothing sounds and symbolizes the connection between humans and nature. Every movement of the shaman with the wayra is not only a physical dance, but also a prayer in movement, a silent dialogue with the invisible. Shamans believe that the sound of wayra can invoke protective spirits, cleanse the aura, and facilitate the patient's spiritual journey during ayahuasca rituals.

The use of the wayra accompanies the entire course of the ceremony from the initial phase, when the sacred drink is "energised", which for shamans translates into activating and recalling "the spirit of the yagé". Subsequently, the ceremony is enriched with an eclectic symphony: sometimes it is the wild music of the Amazon jungle that acts as a backdrop, other times it is the deeply inspired songs of the shaman, known as icaros, that guide the spiritual journey. There is no shortage of moments in which musicians, or "musicos", intertwine so-called medicine music, a fundamental element of the shamanic tradition, into their melodies. Particularly for Colombian shamanic tribes, this music transcends the simple concept of notes and melodies; it transforms into a real language of the soul, which communicates directly with the hearts of the participants and builds a sonic bridge between the tangible and invisible worlds.

Normally, musical instruments are used by the shamans themselves or by their apprentices since it is very important for them to hear their deep meaning. In the context of shamanic ayahuasca rituals, music plays a crucial role, comparable to that of a therapeutic tool in modern medicine, as it serves to facilitate the processes of healing and psychological well-being with similar effectiveness to recognized clinical treatments. In shamanic practice, music, often in the form of chants or sounds produced by instruments such as the wayra, is essential in guiding participants through the ayahuasca experience, considered a form of spiritual healing and introspection.

Scientific research shows that music has beneficial effects on anxiety, depression, pain and fatigue, especially in cancer patients.[8] In this sense, music in ayahuasca rituals could have a similar therapeutic impact, acting as a powerful catalyst for inner journeying and emotional exploration.

Music in ayahuasca rituals, as well as in medicine music, can serve as a powerful emotional tool for coping with stressful situations. Music in these contexts is used to respond to physical, psychological, social and emotional needs, promoting a form of non-pharmacological therapy.[9] Furthermore, the music in these rituals can be considered an equivalent of the music therapy intervention, where a personalized approach guided by a qualified therapist (in this case the shaman or "musician") is fundamental.

---

[8] Reference in the chapter "Bibliographical References"
[9] Reference in the chapter "Bibliographical References"

Shamans use essences and incense to create a sacred atmosphere, especially in the initial stages of the ceremony. These aromatic elements are also used during the ritual to harmonize the environment and, in particular, after the "limpia", to further enhance the purification effect and facilitate a state of increased receptivity and inner openness in the participants.

From a scientific point of view, aromas and perfumes have been shown to influence the psychological and physical state of people. Research in the field of aromatherapy has shown that certain smells can have calming effects, reduce stress and improve mood.[10]These effects are due to the interaction of odors with the limbic system of the brain, the region responsible for emotions and memories.[11]

Additionally, smells can help anchor participants in the experience, providing a sensory reference point that can be calming in times of intense emotion or psychological upset. In this context, aromas serve as a bridge between the physical and spiritual worlds, facilitating a deeper and more meaningful journey.

Out of respect for the Masters and to guarantee the completeness of the information, it is appropriate to specify that what has previously been described represents only a fraction of the shamanic ritual of ayahuasca. There are many other sacred gestures and moments that remain preserved as knowledge reserved for the shamans themselves. In some cases, these aspects may be difficult to explain in a literal way

---

[10]Reference in the chapter "Bibliographical References"

[11]Reference in the chapter "Bibliographical References"

due to their complexity and their profound difference compared to our common knowledge.

In summary, the shamanic ritual of ayahuasca constitutes a perfect example of the harmonious fusion between traditional practices and modern science. This union creates a holistic experience that connects spirituality, science and psychophysical well-being in a single and fascinating context.

In every corner of the world, across different eras and cultures, rituals have always played a fundamental role. They represent sacred bridges between our daily and deeper selves, binding us to what I call 'cosmic energy', a term chosen for its universality, to respect all religions and beliefs. The ritual invites us to enter a sacred space, created not only physically but also internally, where we can reconnect with the most intimate parts of our being.

In my workshops and online courses, I place great emphasis on the importance of dedicating yourself to creating sacred space, even if that only means dedicating a few minutes to meditation each day. Recognizing and honoring these moments allows us to get closer to our True Essence, opening the door to a journey of personal and spiritual discovery. This concept transcends the simple preparation of a physical area: it is an invitation to give value and profound meaning to those moments, to seek a connection with the most genuine version of oneself.

I also highlight the transformative value of taking on the role of guide in these sacred acts, similar to what a shaman or spiritual leader does. This practice is not limited to merely conducting a ceremony; it extends to the importance of distancing oneself from one's Ego. Understanding that it is possible to wear multiple roles and assume different identities, while maintaining a critical distance from them, is crucial. This detachment opens the way to the exploration of new dimensions of the self, to the embodiment of unexplored qualities and potential, encouraging personal growth that goes beyond the limits of the everyday self.

And you, have you ever felt the call of a ritual, or experienced the profound connection that can be created in a sacred space, be it in the Amazon jungle or in the silence of your room?

## Challenges and Revelations

Facing life's challenges can sometimes feel a little like playing a complicated board game without instructions. You can easily lose your bearings, but it is precisely in these moments that the most powerful revelations emerge. Every crisis, large or small, holds invaluable potential for personal growth and renewal. It's like finding a hidden light in a dark room, which, once turned on, illuminates the entire path.

One of the techniques I created, which I use during my shamanic retreats and workshops to explore the journey towards self-mastery, is the 'Ego-Transcendence Practice' which aims to embrace a more balanced and full life.

I was very impressed by the results obtained with James, a successful lawyer, who completely transformed himself, freeing himself from limiting mental chains and discovering an inexhaustible source of creative energy. It's as if he had found the keys to a door that he had always ignored.

In my life too, these practices have worked wonders. I remember a time when I was so overwhelmed by work pressures that I forgot to breathe (almost literally!). With the 'Ego-Transcendence Practice', I rediscovered the art of balancing ambition and serenity, learning that true wealth is a balanced mix of external success and internal peace.

The words contained in these pages are an invitation to travel into your personal spirituality and find that harmony between the material and the spiritual. It's a bit like having a compass to navigate a sea of possibilities, where true abundance is the hidden treasure.

In the depths of shamanic experiences, I rediscovered the meaning of wealth and success. Before, I measured success in terms of material achievements, like an explorer counting his treasures. But now, through shamanic practices and ceremonies, I have begun to see wealth in a completely different light. It's as if I had put on the right glasses and suddenly everything appears clear: true wealth does not lie in possessing, but in knowing how to enjoy what life offers, in flowing with the universe.

Nowadays, in every project I undertake, I realize that I am no longer the one chasing the money; on the contrary, it is as if money itself is looking for me, arriving like old friends knocking on the door unexpectedly. During this journey, I learned to value every moment of the process, moving away from the traditional conception of work to see it rather as a vehicle to manifest my True Essence. This evolution in my vision of prosperity has transformed everyday life into an exciting adventure, where authentic joy comes from establishing deep connections with my interior and with the surrounding environment, navigating a journey that turns out to be both material and spiritual.

## *Shaman's Code: The Ritual*

In the shamanic path, the ritual is a sacred moment, a bridge between the material and spiritual worlds. This code invites you to rediscover the sacred in small things, finding magic and meaning even in the most banal of everyday gestures. Every aspect of the ritual, from dressing to music, has profound meaning and contributes to a more intimate connection with the inner self. In shamanic life, every moment can become sacred, even when you're making your morning coffee or going through that meeting with the boss. This code will guide you to create your own personal ritual, transforming everyday actions into opportunities to celebrate and connect with your deepest self.

## Step 1: Dressing

Start with 'dressing'. Change your outfit or wear a special item like a necklace or bracelet. It could also be a chef's apron full of sauce stains or your lucky sweater. Every item you wear helps transform you into the main character of your daily ritual. Even a simple accessory can serve as a reminder to stay anchored to the present moment, reminding you to live every action with intention and presence. Remember, this ritual is uniquely yours. Choose items that speak to your soul, make you smile or bring you peace. Whether it's a stone collected on a special trip or a pendant given by a close friend, each item you choose adds a personal touch and deeper meaning to your ritual.

This moment represents a transformation, similar to the one you experience every time you get ready for work, for a workout at the gym or for a meeting with friends. It is a way to honor your presence in every moment of the day, to celebrate the sacred in everyday gestures and to remind you that you are the creator of your reality, a shaman of your existence.

## Step 2: Preparing the Space

Choose and prepare your sacred space. Whether it's your desk, with those brightly colored post-its, or the kitchen, with every spice that becomes a magical ingredient, every object helps create a special atmosphere for your ritual. Gather all the elements you will need for your meditation or for any activity you are about to undertake. Consider adding an object that inspires or calms you - a plant, a scented candle, or a photograph that gives you peace of mind.

## Step 3: Music Medicine

Music is your sonic spell. Accompany your ritual with music. Choose medical or meditation music that helps you reconnect with your inner self.

## Step 4: Essences

If you are cooking, let the aromas of the food become your essence. Or, light some incense to transform your office into a temple. These aromas act as catalysts for your inner journey, helping you create an atmosphere of concentration and serenity. If you don't have incense or essences, consider using an essential oil or even just the flavoring of the coffee or tea you're making.

Each part of this ritual will allow you a connection with yourself and the environment around you. When you light incense or listen to music, feel how these elements interact with the space around you, creating a harmony between your inside and the outside world. This connection is a powerful reminder of how we are all intertwined with the universe.

## Step 5: Intention

Set the intention for your ritual. Whether you're meditating, cooking, or preparing for a meeting with your boss, focus on the goal you want to achieve. As you set your intention, remember that the power lies in both the achievement and the journey you take, even if it's just surviving a Monday morning. As you follow these steps, remember that your ritual can and should evolve over time. Listen to your heart and your instincts: if one day you feel the need to modify a passage, add a new element or change the order, trust these intuitions. Your ritual is alive and reflects your personal journey.

## Step 6: Conclusion

Conclude your ritual with a symbolic gesture: it can be specific music, a prayer or simply some words chosen from your heart. Always use the same closing ritual for each of your "ceremonies". Finally, take a moment to appreciate the result you have achieved, even if it has not yet manifested itself. After you conclude the ritual, take a moment to reflect on what you just experienced. Write down any thoughts or feelings that arise, to bring awareness and appreciation to your daily journey.

This ritual is not just a series of steps, but reveals itself as a solemn invitation to celebrate the unrepeatability of one's being. A unique opportunity opens up before you to infuse balance and harmony into the fabric of your existence, a gentle reminder that spirituality can be delicately woven into the everydayness of life. By wearing your 'ritual garb,' whether you're orchestrating a meeting or simply placing dinner on the table, you are elevating an ordinary moment to the sacred. These gestures, simple but profound, become the expression of your spirit and a recognition of the beauty and mystery hidden in the everyday and the familiar.

Heraclitus, the venerable Greek philosopher, proclaimed: 'The path up and down is one and the same.'[12] These words find a profound echo in the practice of shamanic ritual, reminding us that every act of our day, no matter how banal it may seem, is a fragment of a unified spiritual journey.

Through this ritual, every routine is transfigured into an act of pure awareness and living presence. It stands as a reminder that, even in the whirlwind of daily challenges, there is a sanctuary of peace and self-connection, always within our reach. Every gesture is charged with the potential to explore one's personal evolution and to honor the enchantment hidden in every dawn.

Remember, you are the ruler of your destiny, the architect of your spiritual journey. With this ritual, you welcome your most authentic essence and open the doors to a horizon of transformation and rebirth without borders.

---

[12] Reference in the chapter "Bibliographical References"

# Transformative Relationships

*"We do not walk the earth as strangers, but as close relatives."*

~ Native American proverb

## Shaman in the Modern World

My adventure in the following years turned into a fascinating journey, a sort of world tour of the spirit. I led retreats in locations ranging from lush tropical forests to pulsating metropolises, interacting with a kaleidoscope of cultures and meeting hundreds of people, each with a unique and moving story. The role of a shaman in the modern world, I have discovered, is a bit like being a tightrope walker walking a tightrope between two very different worlds.

As an entrepreneur, I admit that embracing the concept of "shaman" has not been a linear path. Initially, it was like wearing a hat that was too big for my head, something that didn't seem to fit the portrait of a businessman I had constructed. My friends watched with a mixture of skepticism and concern, probably wondering if I had replaced my financial predictions with Mayan prophecies. But what I was really doing was navigating a tumultuous sea of internal realignment, trying to make my logical mind coexist with a soul that craved deeper connection.

During the approximately two years I spent within the organization - yes, the very one where I cleaned the bathrooms - I found an inexhaustible source of inspiration. The practice of "integration", introduced by its founder Alberto Varela, has profoundly marked my path, offering me a harmonious balance between rationality and spirituality. In Alberto, I recognized a "Master" for the admiration I had for him, both as the founder of an organization that brought together exceptional talents from around the world, and as an expert guide in navigating the complexities of the soul and mind. His wisdom and extraordinary communication skills made him a unique point of reference, capable of enlightening and inspiring anyone who crossed his path.

My brief experience in this context was deeply inspiring, a period of my life for which I feel immense gratitude, particularly towards Alberto. His recent transition to a higher state of existence reminds me of the preciousness of his teachings and the depth of his impact on my personal journey. His legacy lives on not only through the practices he left behind, but also in the deep sense of gratitude that resides in my heart for the time spent under his guidance.

Within the organization and in the following years, I had the incredible opportunity to work alongside traditional shamans and combine the knowledge of professionals of the caliber of psychologists, psychotherapists, doctors and intellectuals of great importance. From these experiences, I drew inspiration to develop a new technique, which I called "Ego-Transcendence Practice".

The essence of this practice lies in finding harmony between rationality and intuition, it combines the discoveries of neuroscience and quantum physics with psychological approaches, intertwining them with a profound spirituality. It is a journey of personal growth that has its roots in tangible reality, while elevating towards higher spheres of the spirit. Using this "tool", every action, even the smallest, becomes a significant step towards the transcendence of the self and the reconnection with our most intimate essence. It is an exploration of interiority and a true embrace of the entire universe of our being.

The Ego-Transcendence Practice became a beacon guiding participants in my ceremonies and workshops, and even myself, through the turmoil of the modern world. Like dancing in the rain, learning to rejoice in every drop while trying not to slip. Each session, each retreat is one more step in this journey of balance and discovery, which has transformed my vision of life, work and human relationships.

"Shaman in the Modern World" or "The Modern Shaman" is both the title of a chapter in my life and an invitation to explore how everyone can find their own unique balance, embracing both the material and spiritual worlds. It's a story of how to learn to navigate modernity without losing touch with that part of us that resonates with the Earth's ancestral rhythms. And, in some ways, it's also a comedy because - let's face it - sometimes the spiritual journey can have its hilarious moments, especially in trying to illustrate to your companions the essence of a shamanic ritual in the short intervals between a business meeting and the other one.

Thank you, Alberto, for being a radiant light on my path, an encounter that made my soul vibrate!

## The Internal Value

At one of my retreats, I had the opportunity to meet a well-known entrepreneur who we'll call John for privacy reasons - and because it definitely sounds good. His success in business had immersed him completely in a world of numbers, graphs and reports, a language I knew very well. During an Ego-Transcendence Practice session, he took me by surprise with a question: "How can I place true value on myself?"

I decided to play with him by offering him a Hollywood science fiction movie style exercise: "Imagine you only have five minutes of life left, but you are given the opportunity to buy another five to do something special. What would you do with those extra minutes?" After a thoughtful pause, John replied, "I would say goodbye to the people I love." Well, now tell me: "how much are those five minutes worth to you?". At first he regarded it as if it were a simple business transaction;

however, upon reflection for a moment, he ended up assigning an eight-figure value to those five minutes.

Next, we started to break down this figure, almost like a complex recipe. "How much is your ideal annual income?" we divided him by months, days and hours, to discover the value attributed to every moment of his life, including sleep. John's voice changed over the course of the exercise, going from a stiff tone to a deep introspection. When they calculated the value of a single minute of his life (despite the eight figures he indicated), John was surprised and visibly moved. He tried to maintain a businessman's composure, but his struggle to hold back his emotions was evident, as if he wanted to prevent a rebellious tear from slipping down. With this exercise, the goal was to demonstrate the unconscious value we attribute to every passing minute of our lives. Giving it a price in a "system" where everything has an economic value helps us understand how precious every moment is. The result is almost always the same: amazement mixed with profound realization and, inevitably, that usual tear.

A few months later, during a workshop, John confided to me that the exercise had radically changed his perception of life. He had begun to dedicate more time to his family, living every moment with more presence and attention. This new awareness allowed him to appreciate the intrinsic value of every moment of his life, changing his approach towards his loved ones and his daily activities. He confided to me that he sometimes stopped to look at the clock as a minute passed, reflecting: "Incredible, I could have made seven dollars in this minute, but instead I chose to invest it in watching my son chase butterflies, a time that never it is quantifiable in money. Who would have thought that the real profit lies in living in the present moment rather than in numbers?"

Our conversation reminded me that the true value of life is found in relationships, shared moments, and authentic connections. John discovered that true wealth is not found in the numbers of a bank account, but in the smiles of his children, in family evenings, and in the small gestures that make life meaningful. He had learned that measuring success does not mean counting money, but counting the moments that fill the heart with joy.

In this exercise, John has become a living example of how a change in perspective can transform not only one's life but also the lives of those around us. He has learned that being present, giving attention and love are the true indicators of a life well lived. And with this revelation, he discovered that every day is an opportunity to create wealth of a kind that cannot be quantified but only felt and experienced.

## How to be "Present"

The concept of being truly present touched my soul in an unforgettable way. I remember as if it were this moment the moment in which, returning from a shamanic retreat, I saw my son Alessandro, who had recently turned eight, wrapped in the quiet of our home, completely immersed in reading a book. It was an image of pure innocence and profound wisdom, a bridge between worlds through printed words.

From his early years, Alessandro showed a thirst for knowledge that went beyond simple curiosity, which later branched out into a variety of passions and interests. Since he began reading, he has proven to be a voracious reader, immersing himself in books of all genres, including some so complex that they defy even the comprehension of an adult. He possesses the soul of an explorer, determined to travel through the pages of books to discover unknown worlds and unexpected stories. His passion for reading is a flame that still burns today with a rare intensity, a light that illuminates paths of learning and discovery.

That day, moved by an impulse that felt divine, I decided to do something radically simple but profoundly powerful: I sat next to him, choosing to abandon all distractions to immerse myself in the precious "art of just being". At that moment, time seemed to stand still. The outside world, with its incessant demands, vanished, leaving us in a bubble of silent, vibrant intimacy.

And so we remained, for what seemed like an eternity but turned out to be only an hour, connected in a way that words cannot describe. When Alessandro closed the book and turned towards me, his eyes were two stars that shone with pure and uncontaminated emotion. His smile, a ray of sunshine capable of melting away every shadow, was one of the most precious gifts I had ever received. "Thanks dad, it was nice being here with you!" he said, and at that moment, I felt something inside me 'click'.

The realization that washed over me was tumultuous and sweet at the same time. We hugged each other. I could feel his heartbeat against mine.

A flood of emotions overwhelmed me, and suddenly, I understood. I didn't want to be just a "dad" in the traditional sense. I wanted to be an inspirational figure in his life, an example of authenticity and unconditional love. The request for his presence was an invitation to share my time together with the very essence of my soul.

That day became a beacon in my life, illuminating the truth that we often forget: being present is the greatest gift we can offer, to ourselves, to our children and to anyone who crosses our path. True presence, the one that manifests itself wholeheartedly, is the key to weaving deep and meaningful connections. I realized that being a parent is much more than leading; is to inspire. From that moment, I embraced the mission of living with "presence" as my compass, discovering that in the simplest moments lie the deepest truths of existence.

## Alchemy of Connections

My experience has taught me that personal growth is much more than a solitary path; it is a subtle, almost alchemical art of renewing and enriching human connections. Each stage of this peculiar odyssey has renewed my interior, and has infused a new spirit into my relationships, including that with our neighbor. It can be safely said that he has a very particular gift: transforming every discussion with his wife into a nocturnal screaming concert, with colorful dialogues and epithets. Always at night, it is the right time for their family to give educational lessons to their child, with reprimands with a high auditory impact. Yes, just when the rest of the world is trying to embrace dreams, they decide it's the perfect time for a full-blown domestic "opera."

Their performance, which I imagine is performed for my sole enjoyment – because, let's face it, what other audience could there be at that hour? - taught me to appreciate the little joys in life. Now, every time the drama comes to life through their voices, I can't help but smile, thinking, "Behold, my quiet night is enriched with a new chapter!" In its own unique way, this late-night concert added an unexpected dimension to my existence, reminding me that humor can be found in even the most unlikely circumstances.

This transformation we experience is a solitary inner journey, more like a delicate art, a spiritual dance. Every step we take, every movement of our soul, moves in harmony with the universal melody, intertwining our spirit with the souls of those around us. It is like witnessing the dance of the wayra in the hands of the shaman, who delicately moves the leaves around the patient. In this dance, each leaf harmonizes the energy field, similar to how we balance our lives with those close to us, 'healing' any energetic stagnation in our relationships and our souls.

In my journey, I have discovered that relationships are like mirrors that reflect who we are and also who we could become. Do you know when we interact with a person who has the habit of answering "yes, but..." to all our comments? It's actually a way to avoid really listening to us.

I have learned that the most meaningful relationships are those in which we can be authentically ourselves, without masks or pretensions. They are those moments when, sitting in silence with a friend, you don't feel the need to fill every pause with words, but you can simply "be". It's a bit like taking part in a work video conference, impeccable in the visible part, but in reality under the desk we are comfortably in jogging shorts or socks with puppets, indifferent to what others might think if only they could see the picture business suit.

On my exploratory journey of self-discovery, I've realized that the truest and deepest connections blossom in embracing our vulnerability. It is in sharing our fears, hopes and dreams that relationships find their true meaning. Just like a shaman in his ceremony, who empties himself of every thought to become a pure channel of energy, we too, when we free ourselves from our egos and preconceptions, become channels for relational magic. True magic manifests itself in those moments of sincere openness, where unspoken words resonate louder than those spoken, creating a bond that goes beyond simple verbal exchange.

I urge you to meditate on how your personal journey can not only embellish your existence, but also that of the people you love. Remember that every little progress in your personal development represents a treasure that you can give to yourself and others around you.

In the core of the relationships that transform us, we discover that authentic alchemy does not consist in changing others, but in allowing our inner evolution to inaugurate new paths and spaces for sincere and profound connections. It is a delicate art, that of weaving the filaments of our lives with those of others, creating a living fabric of human experiences that nourish the soul.

The power of this alchemy was made clear to me in a special moment with my second son, Riccardo, when he was just two years old. We were on the shoreline with my wife Rossella, and he was immersed in building sand castles with the naturalness of a little architect. One of his skills is creating something surprising out of nothing. As I watched him, I was inspired by his world of innocent genius. He approached me, perhaps to capture my attention, and at that moment, moved by an intuition, I asked him: "Where do you come from? And why did you choose me in particular?"

The response was disarming spontaneity, typical of his tender age. With a meaningful gesture, she pointed to the sea and said, "I'm from there," in a voice that seemed to carry the secrets of a world lost in innocence. Then, fixing me with a look full of affectionate sincerity, she added: "And I chose you because you are the universe of laughter."

These simple words, but full of profound meaning, vibrated in us like the sweetest melody. Rossella, at my side, shook my hand, sharing that indescribable emotion, that sense of complicity that only the words of a child can evoke. The confidence with which she had pointed to the sea had struck us deeply, as if she had revealed an ancient secret, a sacred bond with the infinite.

In that moment, with the sound of the waves in the background and his contagious smile illuminating us, we understood the true essence of our relationships. A child's pure and direct vision of happiness and love made us reflect on the preciousness and privilege of being a parent.

My little one's gaze, a melting pot of trust and affection, reflected the most sincere and profound values we had ever known. His words, pronounced with the naturalness of someone who does not yet know the filter of adult rationality, became for us a beacon and an invitation to live every day with love, joy and presence.

In that embrace, feeling her little body close to mine and Rossella at my side, a wave of emotions overwhelmed me. The purity and authenticity of her words revealed to me that my role as a parent transcended education and protection; it was also a journey of listening, learning and shared growth.

And in that silence, enriched by love and the gentle crashing of the waves, I learned one of the most significant lessons of my life.

Thank you, my children, for choosing me.

### *Relationship Code: Hidden Alchemy*

This exercise is an exploratory adventure into the depths of your relationships, a journey to discover and strengthen the hidden bonds that bind us to others. Like an explorer discovering uncharted lands, he will guide you through the labyrinth of human interactions, revealing hidden treasures of understanding and love. It's designed to transform even the most ordinary moments into occasions of deep connection, generating that spontaneous laughter that warms the heart and that awareness that makes us say "Now, this is what really matters!"

### Step 1: Preparing the Soil

- Choose a quiet, cozy place where you and your connection partner (a family member, friend or colleague) can feel comfortable.

- Eliminate any potential distractions, especially electronic devices, to create a calm and focused environment.

## Step 2: Active Listening and Sharing

- Start a dialogue on a topic of your choice, something that you both find interesting or important.

- When one speaks, the other listens without interrupting or judging, allowing free and authentic sharing.

- You don't need to provide solutions or advice; the goal is to understand and connect.

## Step 3: Moment of Lightness

- During the conversation, insert a funny story or anecdote capable of triggering a collective laugh. For example, you could talk about the time when, out of distraction, you wore two completely different socks all day, or how a failed attempt at making a cake magically transformed into an unusual, but tasty, homemade pizza. These moments of levity are key to lightening the mood and strengthening the bonds between you.

- Laughter is a powerful tool for connection. It manages to open the heart and make the spirit lighter, creating an environment of sharing and intimacy. Knowing how to laugh at ourselves is an art that teaches us not to take ourselves too seriously, thus allowing us to distance ourselves from our Ego and break down the barriers that sometimes separate us from others. This spontaneity and authenticity in interactions enriches everyone's experience, making the moment together even more special and memorable.

**Step 4: Individual Reflection**

- After the conversation, take a moment to personally reflect on the experience.

- Think about what you learned about your partner and how this experience affected your relationship.

**Step 5: Sharing Reflections**

- If you feel comfortable, share your reflections on the experience.

- Express appreciation for sharing and listening to each other.

Through this exercise, you will discover the "hidden alchemy" in your relationships, those deep and meaningful connections that are revealed when we commit to being truly present and open with each other. This practice offers a precious opportunity to rediscover the intrinsic magic in everyday interactions, strengthening the bonds that embellish our existence. More than a simple activity, it is an invitation to cultivate fertile ground for authentic and meaningful relationships, which can enrich every aspect of life. And for those looking for a partner, this can be a way to establish an authentic and deep connection right away.

# Intimate Prosperity

*"The true voyage of discovery consists not in seeking new lands, but in having new eyes."*

~ Marcel Proust

## Identity Beyond Role

In my journey to find balance between spiritual life and financial success, I have understood the crucial importance of piecing together past experiences, thus weaving the rich mosaic of our identity. This journey can be messy, especially when we become overly immersed in our roles, losing sight of our authentic essence. As an entrepreneur, I have experienced this dilemma firsthand, an experience that is not uncommon even among those navigating waters of material prosperity and health.

For many, professional success becomes a mask they wear with pride, but beneath which lies a disturbing question: who am I beyond this role? In exploring this question, I discovered that our identity is a kaleidoscope of experiences, beliefs, and relationships, not an immobile statue on a pedestal of professional achievement. The true essence of an individual lies in his ability to flow and change, just like a river that changes its course, while maintaining its fundamental nature.

This process of self-inquiry is not for the faint of heart. It's a bit like wearing a shirt with the buttons fastened wrong: at first it might seem that everything is going right, but then you realize that something isn't right. And like in that moment of realization, when you decide whether to start over or continue in the hope that no one will notice, even in the journey of self-discovery you find yourself faced with similar choices. This path requires courage, honesty and, sometimes, an ironic smile in the face of our imperfections.

I have integrated the techniques of modern psychology with the teachings of shamanism into my practice, realizing that our identity is a puzzle made up of pieces of different shapes and colors. Some pieces represent our successes and the roles we have taken on, others are childhood memories, emotional experiences, relationships, dreams and aspirations. It is only through careful observation and acceptance of each piece that we can recompose an authentic image of ourselves, an image that celebrates our uniqueness beyond social and professional labels.

Through the journey of self-discovery, we can learn to balance our material aspirations with our spiritual needs, creating a synergy that not only enriches our lives, but also allows us to live with a deeper sense of purpose and satisfaction. It is a path that teaches us to dance to the rhythm of our spirit, while remaining rooted in the earthly reality of our daily existences.

## Synergy of Science and Spirit

In attempting to merge the mysterious paths of shamanism with the rigorous field of modern science, I have discovered a unique approach, a bit like combining the mysticism of a Tibetan monk with the precision of a quantum physicist. This hybrid practice allows us to examine our daily behaviors with both a psychological and neuroscientific lens, recognizing that many physical ailments are rooted in emotional, mental, and spiritual issues.

Based on neuroscience research, we know that the body and mind are intrinsically connected. According to Damasio in "Descartes' Error: Emotion, Reason, and the Human Brain" (1994)[13], emotions and reason play a crucial role in the decision-making process. This implies that physical well-being is deeply intertwined with mental and emotional well-being.

Healing, therefore, requires a holistic approach. A study conducted by Lutz, Greischar, Rawlings, Ricard, and Davidson (2004), published in "Proceedings of the National Academy of Sciences"[14], shows how meditation can change brain activity in a way that improves positive emotion and inner awareness. These findings highlight the

---

[13] Reference in the chapter "Bibliographical References"
[14] Reference in the chapter "Bibliographical References"

importance of treating the individual as a whole, integrating mind, body, emotions and spirit.

This book guides you to integrate such scientific discoveries with shamanic teachings. The synergy between science and spirit is not just theoretical, but a living practice that you can incorporate into your daily life. It's like dancing between two worlds, where logic meets intuition, and analytical thinking merges with spiritual wisdom.

Through this fusion, your healing journey becomes an exploratory adventure, where you not only use your brain and logic, but also your heart and soul. This combination of science and spirituality provides a healing path that is both scientifically grounded and spiritually enriching, opening up new possibilities for your holistic well-being.

## The Roots of Being

Delving deeper into the theme of the synergy between science and spirit, we explore how the conditioning received in childhood, especially in the first seven years, profoundly influences who we are. During this crucial period, key neural connections are formed in your child's brain that can have a long-term impact on their emotional and psychological development.

Developmental psychology studies, such as those by John Bowlby and Mary Ainsworth on attachment theories, have demonstrated how early experiences influence patterns of attachment and behavior in future relationships. Their work, as described in "Patterns of Attachment: A Psychological Study of the Strange Situation"

(Ainsworth et al., 1978)[15], reveals that early interactions with caregivers play a fundamental role in the formation of personality and relationship skills.

Furthermore, neuroscientific research shows how these childhood experiences affect the physical structure of the brain. A study by Teicher et al., "The Neurobiological Consequences of Early Stress and Childhood Maltreatment" (Neuroscience & Biobehavioral Reviews, 2003)[16], reveals how childhood trauma can lead to lasting changes in brain areas linked to emotion and memory.

This knowledge allows you to better understand the roots of your current behaviors. Through a path that combines psychological introspection and spiritual healing techniques, you can begin to work on these deep roots. The book guides you through meditation and reflection exercises, helping you explore and rework these childhood experiences to find greater inner peace and understanding of yourself.

The integration of these practices with scientific knowledge offers a path of healing and holistic understanding, which does not simply treat superficial symptoms, but delves into the depths of your being, offering you the opportunity to profoundly transform your life.

Imagine your mind as a fertile garden. Some plants, grown from seeds planted in your early life, may no longer be necessary or even harmful to your current well-being. The most effective way to deal with these unwanted weeds is to get to their deep roots. Extracting them consciously will allow you to cultivate a healthier and more harmonious

---

[15]Reference in the chapter "Bibliographical References"

[16]Reference in the chapter "Bibliographical References"

internal garden, where new thoughts and more constructive behaviors can flourish.

## Observers of Ourselves

During my travels in the Amazon jungle, I have had the privilege of meeting wise traditional shamans, such as the respected Grand Master Taita Querubin Queta Alvarado. Their ability to connect deeply with nature and access expanded states of consciousness through ancient rituals and practices has been a revelation. The humility of these masters struck me deeply and although I realized that my path would never be that of a traditional shaman, not having been born into a tribe that passed down this knowledge, I learned precious lessons from this experience.

One of the most important aspects I have observed in shamans is the effort to apply shamanic awareness and vision in everyday life, outside of ceremonies. This attempt to maintain a state of "emptiness" or pure observation, which is experienced in shamanic ceremonies, is fundamental. I've learned that it can be a powerful tool in becoming careful observers of ourselves, allowing us to consciously create our reality.

By incorporating these teachings in a practical way into my life, I have experienced significant transformation. This led me to share with my students how they too can apply this wisdom in their daily lives. Through introspection and awareness, we can reveal the deepest aspects of our being and use this knowledge to live a more balanced and satisfying life. Blending these ancient shamanic practices with a modern approach allows us to better explore and understand ourselves, paving the way for greater abundance in all aspects of life.

While I was reviewing the pages of this book, important news reached me, bringing with it a streak of melancholic wonder: Grand Master Taita Querubin, having navigated through a century and a decade of earthly life, had chosen to adopt a new form of existence. For this reason I decided to share with you the magical encounter with him.

Taita Querubin's fame as a master among masters has, over time, crossed the boundaries of the visible and the invisible, gathering around him a circle of disciples, some of whom are today celebrated as luminaries of their generation. One day, as dawn spread lazily over the lands of Putumayo in Colombia, having returned from a night of ceremony under the guidance of one of these masters, an irrepressible impulse pushed me to confide in a friend, Francesco, the premonition I had had: that that same night it was announced to me that I would meet the Grand Master.

Although physical conditions had long precluded Taita Querubin from actively conducting the ceremonies, an indefinable feeling assured me that our paths would cross.

"Yes, it would be nice but I see it as very complicated, if not impossible!". This mixture of skepticism and realism of Francesco was justified considering the advanced age of the Master and the assiduous care of his family. However, fate had in store other plans. After months of delicate attempts on the part of my friend and hopes hanging by a thread, it was Taita Querubin himself who expressed his desire to join us, upsetting all reasonable expectations.

When the long-awaited day finally materialized before our incredulous eyes, I found myself in front of an extremely present man with the clarity of a young man. I welcomed him by offering him the support of my arm which he, with the tenacity typical of free spirits, accepted with gratitude. We walked together at his pace until we covered the last stretch of the road.

I witnessed two nights of extraordinary ceremonies, experiences that exceeded all my expectations, revealing the wide range of human emotions and inspiring in me profound admiration for such mastery. The first night, I asked permission to play one of my songs "Cura Yagé". When I picked up the guitar I took courage from the emotion of being able to play in front of him: "how wonderful!", the Maestro's praise for my modest musical contribution, was a gift that still echoes in my soul.

However, what struck me most occurred during the interval between one ceremony and another. On a particularly sunny afternoon, we found the moment for a deep conversation, punctuated by genuine and spontaneous laughter. I was enveloped by a profound emotion, a mixture of reverence and wonder that only a child can feel when faced with the immensity of the sea or the infinity of the starry sky. In front of him, I felt at the same time tiny, like a grain of sand in the desert, and immense, as if my spirit was expanding beyond the boundaries of the visible. It was as if, in that moment, I had glimpsed the entire Universe reflected in his eyes, a universe in which every question finds an answer and every soul has its place.

Taita knew how to laugh, this exchange steeped in ancient wisdom and laughter that echoed with the genuineness of shared moments, taught me that life, in its purest essence, is a journey of discovery. A path of initiation in which every encounter, every word, every look can reveal a fragment of that mystery we seek. Thanks to that afternoon, I understood that the path of the spirit knows no boundaries except those that we impose on ourselves and that, at any moment, we can choose to go beyond them, guided by the light of knowledge and the love that connects everything.

"This night, prepare yourselves," he said, looking at me and Francesco, "because I will offer you healing." We immediately understood its importance because in shamanic tribes, receiving this ritual from the Grand Master is considered a special event and a great honor. The physical and emotional healing effects I felt made me realize that his power was far beyond an earthly dimension. He had freed up space in my soul.

Thank you, Grand Master, for the journey we shared and the lessons we taught, a legacy that will continue to illuminate my path and that of many others. Safe travels, Master, in your new state of being!

### *Prosperity Code: the shamanic void*

Congratulations on making it this far on your journey! And I have to admit, despite my numerous digressions about my personal history which, I know, have made you roll your eyes several times and think, "Who cares?" Now it's really time to put into practice everything you have patiently learned by reading these pages and playing with the proposed "codes". Prepare to explore the state of "shamanic emptiness," a condition of consciousness as powerful as it is mysterious, where mind and heart synchronize like an old couple finishing each other's sentences. And let's not forget to activate the energy center in the solar plexus, yes, that very area above the stomach where you usually hear the rumblings when you skip breakfast. In this state, open to infinite possibilities and perhaps even a few snacks, you will become a conscious observer of your past, present and those potential futures that you have only dreamed of until now. Combine the wisdom of ancient shamanic teachings with modern scientific discoveries about the coherence between heart and mind, and start walking towards a more balanced and even more prosperous life.

## Step 1: Preparation and Centering

- Well, remember that "personal ritual" you put together with the "shaman's code"? I hope you haven't forgotten it in some dusty corner of your mind. It's time to take it out of the drawer!

- Take a seat in your "sacred" place.

- Sit or lie down comfortably but remain Present!

- Breath deeply. Let each breath be like a wave that carries you away from the chaos of the day. Imagine that every sigh releases a little piece of that tension that you've been carrying around for... well, for too long.

## Step 2: Mind-Heart Coherence

- Focus on your breathing and imagine a flowing connection between your heart, mind and solar plexus.

- Visualize an energy that unites them, bringing you into a state of coherence and tranquility. Feel the heat intensify at these points.

## Step 3: Access the Shamanic Void

- In this calm state, open your mind to the concept of "emptiness," a space of infinite possibilities.

- Let go of thoughts and allow yourself to enter a state of pure being and observation.

## Step 4: Contemplation of Possibilities

- While you are in this state of emptiness, reflect on the infinite possibilities of your life.

- Consider how each decision and thought can affect your path.

## Step 5: Set an Intent

- With clarity and determination, set an intention for what you want to manifest in your life.

- Let this intention take root deeply in your being.

## Step 6: Return and Integration

- Slowly, return to ordinary awareness.

- Reflect on how to apply this awareness in your daily life, maintaining a connection with the shamanic void.

Through this exercise, you will discover your ability to co-create your reality. Consistent practice will allow you to use the power of the shamanic void to create a life of balance, prosperity and satisfaction, reminding you that you are the creator of your life experience and that every moment is an opportunity for growth and transformation.

# The Future of Value

*Nothing is more powerful than being yourself!*

~ Antonio Siano

## Balance between Spiritual and Material

In my journey to find balance between spirituality and material goods, I discovered a fundamental truth: we don't have to choose between our inner well-being and outer success. It taught me that true value lies in cultivating a conscious and meaningful presence in the lives of those around us.

Material wealth and spiritual growth can coexist in harmony, enriching each other. In my life, achieving balance between these two dimensions has become a fundamental pillar. Today I recognize the importance of the comfort and security that money can offer, together with the essential value of inner wealth.

This awareness has led me to share my knowledge in a practical way, through tangible examples and inspiring stories that demonstrate how it is possible for everyone to find their own path to a balanced existence, where the pursuit of happiness, health and abundance material intertwine. A path that can concern both the achievement of external objectives and the awakening and valorisation of our internal potential.

I have learned that by becoming conscious creators of our reality, we can attract prosperity in all its forms. For me it means, in addition to earning money, also attracting meaningful relationships, enriching experiences and a sense of personal satisfaction that can permeate every aspect of our lives. A key to a truly prosperous and meaningful life.

## Prosperity Beyond Money

The path to achieving a more balanced approach to prosperity has taught me that chasing money alone can lead to an unnecessary sacrifice for one's mental and physical health. True prosperity follows the path of our personal and spiritual growth.

By aligning your deepest values with material goals, you create a natural and constant flow of abundance. The richness of relationships, the joy of small things, and the satisfaction of living a meaningful life are the true essence of prosperity. They can enrich every aspect of our lives and help us discover the balance between material well-being and inner growth.

The story of Katy and her husband Albert is a touching example of this truth.

"I don't know what to do anymore," Katy began in a phone call, her voice laced with desperation. "We visited all the most renowned hospitals in the world."

His confession touched me deeply, revealing a mix of pain and lost hope that only a parent facing a child's illness can feel.

"Katy, the first step is to believe in therapies and doctors," I replied, trying to instill courage. "But there is something deeper we need to address, something that concerns you and your husband."

Thus, the luxury of private jet travel and a life of extreme comfort that Katy and Albert knew well clashed with the simplicity of the retreat we organized. They were three days of exploring not only the intricacies of their lives but also their souls.

"We never learned to really enjoy what we have. It was always a rush towards the next goal, never stopping to enjoy the moment," confided Katy, sitting in front of me with her hands intertwined with Albert's.

Albert, with shining eyes, nodded: "These days have opened my eyes. I understood that true wealth is here, in our being together, in the support we can give each other."

Through intense inner work and the adoption of various practices and techniques, some of which are detailed in this book, we delved into the roots of their childhood experiences. This path allowed us to "unlock" those repetitive behavioral patterns that had left a significant mark on their existence and that of their family, in particular on their young son.

The result of this journey? About seven years later, Katy regularly updates me on how their relationship has improved, become deeper and more communicative, and how their son, now a teenager, is doing much better, living a life wrapped in the love of his family.

Katy and Albert have also founded a charity to help families facing the same challenges, extending their prosperity far beyond the material dimension.

By sharing their story, I hope I have conveyed the depth of their journey and the hope that comes with it. It is an invitation to rediscover the small joys, the bonds that unite us and the personal growth that enriches us, demonstrating that true prosperity goes beyond money.

## Personal and Global Sustainability

Through these pages, I have shared a fragment of the lessons and techniques that have marked my path. I didn't become a saint, or a guru, or anything like that. I am a human being, just like you, who makes mistakes and faces failures. However, what has really changed for me is how quickly I now recognize my mistakes: what once would have taken months to fully understand and accept now happens in seconds. This speed of realization is the result of sincere honesty with oneself, an incredibly powerful tool.

The journey to a life full of abundance and deep relationships has taught me that sustainability is not only an environmental concept, but also a fundamental principle for our personal growth. Understanding and balancing our material and spiritual needs is crucial to maintaining our mental and physical health, avoiding depleting our internal resources.

In parallel, global sustainability requires a respectful approach towards our planet, which involves protecting the environment together with promoting a sustainable economy and communities for future generations. In this context, relationships play a key role. A strong support network, built on meaningful connections, not only fosters our personal growth but also stimulates a positive impact on the environment and society.

Through integrating shamanic practices and sustainable perspectives into everyday life, we can live abundantly without sacrificing our relationships or the health of the planet. This path teaches us that it is possible to be prosperous and responsible at the same time, helping to build a more balanced and sustainable world.

If you have been captured by these pages and my words, know that there is much more to discover and experience. The transformative experiences described are just the beginning. Continue to explore your inner quest, because the true value of life lies in your ability to become your own master and co-create your reality.

I invite you to reflect not only on what you have read, but also to connect with your personal experiences and see how you can integrate these teachings into your daily life. The desire for happiness, health and abundance is universal, and you have the power to make it happen. Never stop searching, learning and growing.

## Conscious Creation of the Future

How do we say goodbye after this long dialogue in search of ourselves, where we have been in deep connection? Just as I would do up close: with the story of an encounter that taught me something. Among the many stories of people with whom I have been lucky enough to intertwine my path is Michael, but first I would like to update you on Marion. The love of music has opened new doors of her soul and I am happy to inform you that a special person has entered her life, a soul in perfect harmony with hers. Whenever she gets the opportunity, she grabs her guitar and dedicates a song to her significant other, weaving together melodies that glorify their love. Her notes, emanating directly from her heart, pay homage to the unifying power of music, demonstrating how it can become a universal language of connection and deep affection.

In this rhythm of life, at a certain point a few years ago Michael's energy entered and life took me on the path of Michael, a young musician of about twenty-five years old, gifted with extraordinary talent. His voice had the power to touch the soul of anyone who listened to him, but a terrible disease threatened to extinguish that precious gift forever, putting his vocal chords at risk. Michael came from a family of successful entrepreneurs, but the tormented relationship with his father seemed to have profoundly affected him, influencing his ability to express himself. A blockage that manifested itself right in the throat, seat of the vocal cords and the energy center linked to communication.

A particular moment has remained indelibly imprinted in my memory. During that retreat that changed Michael's life I approached him and he looked at me with eyes that reflected a sea of emotions held back for too long. I had the impression that his gaze was about to cross an invisible threshold, ready to leave that enormous weight behind.

"What do you really want, Michael?" I asked him, infusing as much calm and support as I could through my voice. The words floated in the space between us, filled with palpable anticipation.

With a sigh that seemed to drag with it years of unchosen silences, Michael replied, his voice a thin but clear thread, "I want my soul to sing... I want to be true, to show the world my deepest essence." His words were a whisper, but they echoed with the force of a liberating cry.

I told him, placing a hand on his shoulder in brotherly support, "It's time to let go of everything that's weighing you down. Here and now, Michael. Free your voice, free yourself."

Tears began to flow down her face, first timidly, then in an unstoppable flow. They were not just tears of pain, but of revelation, of rebirth. Michael cried, and we all cried with him, united in a moment of pure humanity and sharing. That cry became a symbol of our collective journey towards truth and authenticity.

Since then, Michael has embarked on a journey of continuous evolution and discovery, exploring the depths of his soul through music. Each new album by him is a chapter in this exploration, a gift that touches the soul of the listener, reminding us that every voice, when authentic, can resonate deeply in the hearts of others.

Michael's story is a powerful reminder that the motto "Your Future is Now" is already realized deep within your soul. We can learn from him that the deepest transformation begins when we choose to face and release what holds us back, allowing our purest essence to shine and sing, free, into the world.

Thank you for accompanying me on this narrative journey. Writing this book was a journey of personal reflection for me, further confirmation of the extraordinary adventure that is life. I have imbued these pages with the energy of harmony and love, convinced that they have reached you, perhaps not to your conscious mind, but certainly to your soul, which is always listening.

I encourage you to never give up, to pursue your truth every day, to let your inner voice guide your path.

Repeat the codes to unlock your potential, which I have proposed, and constantly seek inner evolution. As we saw in 'The Shaman's Code: The Ritual", the daily application of these principles has the power to transform your reality and profoundly change your perception of it.

And never forget: a genuine smile and a heartfelt laugh are incomparable allies on this magnificent journey of yours!

I invite you to become the modern shaman of your life and I want to make one thing clear: I am not suggesting that you turn into the kind of shaman who, sitting at a restaurant table, takes the wayra out of the bag to "energize" the salad, causing a such an extraordinary spectacle that even the waiter stops to take notes on the "new spiritual seasoning". Nor am I proposing that you recite financial success formulas to your corporate balance sheets, expecting the red numbers to magically turn to black. Rather, the journey I propose to you is to tune into your intuition and the energies that surround you, in every aspect of daily life, without necessarily resorting to such... exotic external gestures.

Remember, the greatest power lies in the simplicity of your daily actions, the authenticity of your being, and the ability to laugh at yourself, especially when you catch yourself contemplating whether your houseplant's aura needs a little sprucing up. ' of "energy cleansing" with the wayra.

When you need a reminder, a sign, or just a laugh, come back to these pages. Don't think of them as just ink on paper; these are real instructions for navigating the jungle of life. And now, I see you raise an eyebrow, asking, "Can a guy who calls himself 'the modern shaman' really help me find the path to a better life? Really, Antonio?" Well, now it's your turn. He becomes the shaman of your path, creator of your destiny. This book is just the beginning: the real adventure is all in your hands.

This is your epic, O shaman of our times, and the grand epilogue... that, my dear, is yours to write.

Aslepay and have a good journey!

# Bibliographical references


1. Ferriss, T. (2017). Tribe of Mentors: Short Life Advice from the Best in the World. Houghton Mifflin Harcourt.

2. Orwell, G. (1949). 1984. Part 2, Chapter 9. Retrieved from https://www.allgreatquotes.com/nineteen-eighty-four-95/

3. Norman Vincent Peale, 'The Power of Positive Thinking' APA: Peale, N. V. (1952). The Power of Positive Thinking.

4. Alfieri, V. (1804). Life of Vittorio Alfieri from Asti, Written by Himself.

5. Malsert, J., Palama, A., & Gentaz, E. (2020). This study focused on the development of emotional facial perception in children of different ages, exploring the emergence of an emotional other-race effect. Batty, M., & Taylor, M. J. (2006). Their research investigated the development of emotional face processing during childhood. Lemerise, E. A., & Arsenio, W. F. (2000). This work proposed an integrated model of emotion processes and cognition in social information processing. Crick, N. R., & Dodge, K. A. (1994). They reviewed and reformulated social information-processing mechanisms in children's social adjustment. Barrett, L. F., & Satpute, A. B. (2013). Their research contributed to the understanding of large-scale brain networks in affective and social neuroscience. Nook, E. C., et al. (2018). This study examined the nonlinear development of emotion differentiation, highlighting that granular emotional experience is low in adolescence.

6. Napoleon Hill: "Think and Grow Rich" APA: Hill, N. (1937). Think and Grow Rich. Wallace D. Wattles: "The Science of Getting Rich" APA: Wattles, W. D. (1910). The Science of Getting Rich. Ralph Waldo Emerson: "Self-Reliance" APA: Emerson, R. W. (1841). Self-Reliance. William Walker Atkinson: "Thought Vibration or the Law of Attraction in the Thought World" APA: Atkinson, W. W. (1906). Thought Vibration or the Law of Attraction in the Thought World. Eckhart Tolle: "The Power of Now" APA: Tolle, E. (1997). The Power of Now.

7. Beversdorf, D. Q., et al. (2007). Beta-adrenergic modulation of cognitive flexibility during stress. Journal of Cognitive Neuroscience, 19, 468–478.

8. Beversdorf, D. Q. (2018). Stress, pharmacology, and creativity. In The Cambridge Handbook of the Neuroscience of Creativity.

9. Beversdorf, D. Q. (2019). Neuropsychopharmacological regulation of performance on creativity-related tasks. Current Opinion in Behavioral Sciences, 27, 55–63. Bower, J. E., & Kuhlman, K. R. (2023). Psychoneuroimmunology: An Introduction to Immune-to-Brain Communication and Its Implications for Clinical Psychology. Annual Review of Clinical Psychology, 19, 331-359. doi: 10.1146/annurev-clinpsy-080621-045153. Available at: https://pubmed.ncbi.nlm.nih.gov/36791765/

10. Black, D. S., & Slavich, G. M. (2016). Mindfulness meditation and the immune system: a systematic review of randomized controlled trials. Annals of the New York Academy of Sciences, 1373(1), 13-24. doi: 10.1111/nyas.12998. Bennett, D. (2021). Meditation

brings robust immune system activation, UF Health researchers find. University of Florida Health. Retrieved December 14, 2021. Available at: https://ufhealth.org/news/2021/meditation-brings-robust-immune-system-activation-uf-health-researchers-find

11. Bradt, J., Dileo, C., Magill, L., & Teague, A. (2016). Music interventions for improving psychological and physical outcomes in people with cancer - PubMed. Cochrane Database of Systematic Reviews. Jorgie Ann Contreras. (2022). Music as Medicine: A Concept Analysis - PubMed. Creative Nursing. https://pubmed.ncbi.nlm.nih.gov/36411048/ Zhang, J. M., Wang, P., Yao, J. X., Zhao, L., Davis, M. P., Walsh, D., & Yue, G. H. (2012). Music interventions for psychological and physical outcomes in cancer: a systematic review and meta-analysis - PubMed. Support Care Cancer.

12. National Cancer Institute. (n.d.). Aromatherapy and Essential Oils (PDQ®)–Patient Version. Retrieved from National Cancer Institute website. Cho, M. Y., Min, E. S., Hur, M. H., & Lee, M. S. (2009). The effects of aromatherapy on stress and stress responses in adolescents. Journal of Korean Academy of Nursing, 39(3), 357-365. Retrieved from PubMed. Jimbo, D., Kimura, Y., Taniguchi, M., Inoue, M., & Urakami, K. (2009). Effect of aromatherapy on patients with Alzheimer's disease. Psychogeriatrics, 9(4), 173-179. Retrieved from PubMed.

13. Heraclitus. (circa 500 B.C.). Fragments. In Diels, H., & Kranz, W. (Eds.), Die Fragmente der Vorsokratiker (Vol. 1). Weidmannsche Verlagsbuchhandlung.

14. Damasio, A. R. (1994). "Descartes' Error: Emotion, Reason, and the Human Brain". New York: G.P. Putnam's Sons.

15. Lutz, A., Greischar, L. L., Rawlings, N. B., Ricard, M., & Davidson, R. J. (2004). "Long-term meditators self-induce high-amplitude gamma synchrony during mental practice". Proceedings of the National Academy of Sciences, 101(46), 16369-16373.

16. Ainsworth, M. D. S., Blehar, M. C., Waters, E., & Wall, S. (1978). "Patterns of Attachment: A Psychological Study of the Strange Situation". Hillsdale, NJ: Lawrence Erlbaum.

17. Teicher, M. H., Andersen, S. L., Polcari, A., Anderson, C. M., Navalta, C. P., & Kim, D. M. (2003). "The Neurobiological Consequences of Early Stress and Childhood Maltreatment". Neuroscience & Biobehavioral Reviews, 27(1-2), 33-44.

# Appendix: Join the Journey!

Hello, dear traveler of the inner world! If the pages of this book have touched you, the journey does not end here. There's a whole universe of exploration and growth waiting for you, and I'm excited to share even more tools for your journey.

**Website and Guided Meditations:** Visit my web-site https://antoniosiano.com to to access free guided meditations. They are perfect for deepening your practice and bringing you into new states of awareness.

**Social Media:** Follow me on social media for daily updates, tips and a good dose of inspiration. You will find posts full of positive energy, announcements about my events, and much more.

**Podcasts:** If you love listening to stories and insights on the go, don't miss my podcast "The Awakening Podcast" available on YouTube, Spotify, Apple Podcasts, Google Podcasts and many other digital platforms. It's a mix of wisdom, life stories, and a pinch of shamanic humor!

**Music Medicine:** Do you want to add a magical touch to your day? Listen to my medicine music songs, available on spotify, apple, amazon, and many others. It's like a caress for the soul and a booster for your spirit.

**Online Course:** For an even deeper dive into the world of modern shamanism, check out my online course available on the site https://antoniosiano.com. It is a unique opportunity to learn the practices and perspectives that have enriched my journey.

**Exclusive Community:** Join our online community to connect with other like-minded travelers. You will have access to special discounts, exclusive webinars and much more. Sharing with travel companions can make the difference in your journey.

**Let's stay connected:** My mission is to support you on your journey of growth and transformation. Remember, you are not alone on this journey. Together, we can explore the uncharted territories of the soul and unlock our limitless potential.

Thank you for being part of this shamanic journey. Remember, every step you take is a step towards your True Essence. And I will be here to celebrate your every success.

With much love and shamanic laughter